DOING BUSINESS IN VIETNAM

James W. Robinson

WITHDRAWN

P **Prima Publishing**
P.O. Box 1260
Rocklin, CA   95677

© 1995 by James W. Robinson

All rights reserved. No part of this book may be reproduced or transmitted in any form or by any means, electronic or mechanical, including photocopying, recording, or by any information storage or retrieval system, without written permission from Prima Publishing, except for the inclusion of quotations in a review.

Legal consultation for *Doing Business in Vietnam* was provided by Thomas J. Schwarz, senior partner of Skadden, Arps, Slate, Meagher & Flom, and Eugene Matthews, president of Ashta International, Inc.

Production and composition by A-R Editions, Inc.
Cover design by The Dunlavey Studio, Sacramento.

Library of Congress Cataloging-in-Publication Data

Robinson, James W., 1954–
    Doing business in Vietnam / James W. Robinson.
      p.   cm.
    Includes index.
    ISBN 1-55958-591-9
      1. Industrial promotion—Vietnam. 2. Investments, Foreign—Vietnam. I. Title.
    HC444.Z9I537 1994
    330.9597'044—dc20   94-13044
                                                                                          CIP

95 96 97 RRD 10 9 8 7 6 5 4 3 2 1
Printed in the United States of America

How to Order:
Single copies may be ordered from Prima Publishing, P.O. Box 1260BK, Rocklin, CA 95677; telephone (916) 632-4400. Quantity discounts are also available. On your letterhead, include information concerning the intended use of the books and the number of books you wish to purchase.

Contents

Acknowledgments xi
Map of Vietnam xiii

Part One
The New Vietnam: Asia's Next Tiger

Chapter 1 Introducing... "Country X" 3

Chapter 2 *Doi Moi:* What It Means to Vietnam, What It Means to You 9
An Embargo We Thought Would Never End 10
The Embargo Wasn't the Biggest Hurdle
   for International Business! 12
From Disaster to *Doi Moi* 13
The Birth of *Doi Moi:* From Small Steps to Giant Leaps 14
Doi Moi in the Marketplace 15
Is *Doi Moi* Here to Stay? 18
What *Doi Moi* is Not 19
Vietnam Today 23
   Country Profile 23
   Political Profile 24
   Economic Profile 25
Vietnam's Mixed Economy 26

Chapter 3 Vietnam: A World of Opportunities 29
Newsreel: The "Mad Scramble" in Vietnam 30
Where Is the Money Going Today? 31

The "Official" Priorities: What the Vietnamese
   Government Wants   34
Special Note: Tapping into International Lending
   and Aid   37
Opportunities by Region   38
   Ho Chi Minh City and the South   40
   Hanoi and the North   41
   Da Nang and the Central Region   41
Opportunities Sector by Sector   42
   Infrastructure   42
   Construction Materials and Equipment   43
   Manufacturing   44
   Hotels and Tourism   45
   Airlines, Airports, and Airplanes   46
   Computers and Information Technology   47
   Telecommunications   47
   Motor Vehicles and Automotive Parts   48
   Agribusiness   48
   Consumer Products   49
   Entertainment, Sports, and Leisure Activities   50
   Oil and Other Natural Resources   50
   Services   51
   Other Services   52

**Chapter 4 How to Do Business in Vietnam:
            A Step-by-Step Plan   53**
The First Steps: How to Get Started   55
The Next Step: Opening a Representative Office   59
Going Further: Five Approaches to Doing Business
   in Vietnam   61
   Business Cooperation Contract   63
   Joint Venture   63
   100% Foreign-Owned Enterprise   64
   Build-Operate-Transfer (B.O.T.)   65
   Export Processing Zone   65
Forging Ahead: Completing the Business Plan
   and Application Process   66
      Partners   67

Contents   v

       Land   67
       The Application Process   68

Chapter 5 How to Trade in Vietnam   71
    Insignificant Trade—Up to Now   72
    Doi Moi in the International Trade Arena   73
    A Rock and a Hard Place: High Tariffs and Smuggling   74
    Vietnamese May Like American Products More Than
       Americans Do!   76
    Understanding the Vietnamese Consumer   77
    Don't Overlook Selling to the Sellers   80
    Not All Trade Opportunities Have "Sex Appeal"   80
    Marketing and Distribution in Vietnam   81
    Getting Paid   83
    How to Register Trademarks   84
    Eventually, Trade Must Become a Two-Way Street   87
    Steps and Strategies for Trade with Vietnam   88
       Some Important Questions   88
       A Vietnam Trade Checklist   89
       Stages of Involvement: How Dirty Do You Want
         to Get Your Hands?   90

**Chapter 6 Understanding the Vietnamese
          Business Culture   93**
    Names   94
    Dressing for Business in Vietnam   96
    Conduct and Approach in Meetings   97
    Smoking and Drinking   99
    A Woman's Perspective   100
    Relationships   101
    Following Through   101
    Equal Treatment versus Condescension   102
    Talking Politics and Personal Views   102
    Is It Saigon or Ho Chi Minh City?   103
    The North-South Split   104
    Face   105
    Patience-Persistence-Perseverance   106
    Change, Flexibility, and Pragmatism   107

Chapter 7 Problems and Pitfalls   109
    The Legal System   110
    Bureaucracy, Red Tape, and Roving Regulations   111
    Corruption   113
    Partners and Their Promises   115
    The Physical and Financial Infrastructure   116
    High Costs and Burdensome Taxes   117
    Backlash Back Home   119

Chapter 8 Challenges and Opportunities for Overseas Vietnamese and the Companies Who Hire Them   121
    Attitudes of Overseas Vietnamese Are Changing   122
        Family Visits   123
        The Passage of Time and the Ascension of a New Generation   123
        Economic Decline in the United States and the Ascension of Southeast Asia   124
        Love of Country   124
    Attitudes of the Vietnamese Government   125
    Considerations for Companies Hiring Overseas Vietnamese   127
    Considerations for Overseas Vietnamese   130
    Opportunities for Overseas Vietnamese   132

Part Two
The Doing Business in Vietnam Resource Guide

Chapter 9 Guide to Business Travel in Vietnam   137
    Before You Go   138
        Visas   138
        How to Get There   140
        Hotel Reservations   140
        What to Pack, What to Bring, and the Color of Your Money   142
    Arriving in Vietnam   143
        Immigration and Customs   143
        Airport Transfers   145

Contents   **vii**

       Hotel Considerations   145
       Getting Around   149
       Safety on the Streets   151
       Business Services   151
       Language and Communication   152
       Telephone Service   152
       Time   153
       Electricity   153
       Business Hours   153
       National Holidays   154
       Water   154
       Health   155
       Business Entertainment   155

Chapter 10 Twelve Interesting Things to Do in Your Free Time   159

Chapter 11 Sample Itinerary for Your Exploratory Mission   167
   Introductory Trip to Vietnam   168
       Saturday   168
       Sunday   168
       Monday   169
       Tuesday   169
       Wednesday   170
       Thursday   170
       Friday   170
       Saturday   171
       Sunday   171

Chapter 12 Directory of Organizations That Can Help You   173
   In the United States   174
   In Hong Kong   177
   In Thailand   180
   In Vietnam   180
   Selected Trading Companies in Vietnam   184
   Final Note: U.S. Government Assistance in Vietnam   187

Chapter 13 Directory of Government Offices and Current Officials 189
Senior National-Level Officials 190
Ministries and Ministerial-Level Agencies 191
Major People's Committees 196
Other Useful Numbers in Hanoi 197
Other Useful Numbers in Ho Chi Minh City 199

Chapter 14 Information Resources 201

Chapter 15 Examples of Licensed Projects in Vietnam 205

Chapter 16 List of U.S. Firms with a Presence in Vietnam 213
U.S. Companies Licensed to Open Representative Offices 213
List of Companies Exhibiting at Vietnamerica Expo '94 215

Chapter 17 Doing Business in Vietnam: The Bottom Line 221
Ten Myths about Doing Business in Vietnam 222
Ten Realities about Doing Business in Vietnam 222

Appendix A Vietnam's Foreign Investment Law and Key Amendments 225

Appendix B Sample Application Forms for Doing Business in Vietnam 265
Representative Office 266
Business Cooperation License 267
Joint Venture License 269
    Guidance for a Joint Venture Contract and Charter as Issued by the State Committee for Cooperation and Investment 270
100% Foreign-Owned Enterprise License 272
Contents of the Feasibility Study 273

Sources 275
Index 283
About the Author 287

Acknowledgments

Many people helped me with this book, and I am deeply grateful.

Landy Eng in Hong Kong has always been a great "doer," but for me he proved to be a great teacher.

Hung Manh Hoang, who assists Vietnamese refugees in Hong Kong, provided creative research and unique personal perspectives about Vietnam. His counsel and friendship are always appreciated.

I would also like to express my gratitude to publisher Ben Dominitz for giving me yet another wonderful opportunity and to the staff at Prima Publishing, especially Jennifer Basye Sander, Andi Reese Brady, and Karen Blanco, for their assistance. Thanks also to California Attorney General Dan Lungren for his understanding and patience.

Others generously shared their knowledge and personal experiences with me, and I thank them all:

In Hong Kong: David Bagnall; Frank Martin, president of the American Chamber of Commerce; Paul Ho, chairman of Pilkon Development Company; Robin Chiu and Felia Chu of the California Trade and Investment Office; Peter Yu, chairman of Jet Air; Shawna Stonehouse, managing director of Infocus; Thomas J. Schwarz of Skadden, Arps, Slate, Meagher & Flom; Eugene Matthews, president of Ashta International, Inc.; Kathleen Charlton of Ashta International, Inc.; Fred Burke of Baker & McKenzie; Tim Shephard of the State of Maryland Center; John Harvey of Ernst & Young; and Mr. Soojin Lee and William Hui-Bon-Hoa of American Express.

In Vietnam: Julian Do in Da Nang; Dr. Pham Khac Chi and his staff at the Foreign Investment Service Company; Henry Ha, Saigon Star Hotel; Tran Quoc Dung from Saigontourist; Michael Scown of Russin & Vecchi; Tran Thien Cuong of the Vietnam Chamber of Commerce and Industry; Dinh Van Hoi of Vietnam's Ministry of Trade; Tran Thien Tu of the People's Committee of Ho Chi Minh City; Tran Dinh Ha of the Ministry of Construction; Nguyen Xuan Phong, director of the America's Department, Ministry of Foreign Affairs; Le Nghia Vu, director of the Materials Trading and Building Materials Import-Export Company; and Mr. Nguyen Van Canh.

Thanks also to Greg Mignano, Duc Dinh Nguyen, Dave Puglia, Rick Reidy, Gonejanart Rodbhajon, and Jo Wood for their support and friendship and for holding things together.

Finally, I thank Duc Huu Nguyen for all he has done to help me understand his country, culture, and people and what it means to reinvent yourself in a strange new world. This book could not have been written without him.

CHINA
Lao Cai
Dien Bien Phu
HANOI
Hai Phong
LAOS
Vinh
Gulf of Tonkin
VIETNAM
Quang Tri
Hue
South China Sea
Da Nang
THAILAND
Pleiku
CAMBODIA
Nha Trang
Da Lat
Cam Ranh
Can Tho
Vung Tau
Ho Chi Minh City
Gulf of Thailand
0 km 200

Part One
The New Vietnam:
Asia's Next Tiger

1

INTRODUCING... "COUNTRY X"

On February 3, 1994, President Bill Clinton symbolically ended the American war in Vietnam by lifting the trade embargo that had been in place for nearly two decades after the fall of Saigon.

Five hours later, Pepsi fired the first shots in a new war in Vietnam—a cola war.

A giant replica of a soda can was displayed in the heart of what is now called Ho Chi Minh City, suspended under red banners celebrating the sixty-fourth anniversary of the Community Party of Vietnam! T-shirts and hats bearing the Pepsi logo were handed out to eager city residents. Even more welcome were the free samples of the first "product" to roll off the assembly line of a local bottling plant with whom Pepsi had already signed a joint venture. The plant was ready because Pepsi syrup had been flown in from Bangkok earlier in the week as speculation about lifting the embargo grew.

In Hanoi, a young American business consultant hung the U.S. and Vietnamese flags from his office window and threw an all-night party in a city that usually shuts down by 9:00 P.M. Determined not to be outdone by its rival for long, within a few days Coca-Cola blanketed Hanoi with its own banners. Under the familiar Coke logo, the banner read, "It's good to see you again!"

Why the excitement? Why Vietnam?

To most Americans, Vietnam is not a country, a people, or a marketplace but a war. To many, the word *Vietnam* has come to mean brutality, defeat, and futile foreign adventurism. To some, *Vietnam* might as well be a four-letter word.

In the 1980s, opponents of President Ronald Reagan's policy on Nicaragua adopted as their slogan, "No Vietnam in Central America." It needed no explanation.

In the early 1990s, when President George Bush rallied Americans to the cause of freeing Kuwait from Saddam Hussein, he did so by repeatedly promising, "This will not be another Vietnam." Everyone knew what he meant.

No one can presume to tell a Vietnam veteran, the family of a missing loved one, or a Vietnamese refugee who escaped tyranny in a leaky boat that it is time to forgive and forget. They must make their own peace in their own time. But for the vast majority, it is time to move on. It *is* time to see Vietnam not just as a war but as a country, a people, and a marketplace of great opportunity.

We know so much and yet so little about this country. Painful images are seared in our minds, yet Vietnam remains remote and mysterious. Well, try to forget for a moment that we are speaking of Vietnam. What would you say if I told you that with the stroke of President Clinton's pen on February 3, 1994, a new international market, call it Country X, had been created? This country could be characterized as follows:

- Country X is the thirteenth most populous nation in the world with 71 million people and a projected 80 million by the year 2000.

Introducing... "Country X"

- Country X has an abundant, highly literate, hard-working workforce that works six days a week for $30 to $35 per month.

- Country X is rich in natural resources including minerals, forests, and offshore oil and has a 1,600-mile coastline with tremendous potential for the development of tourism and sea products.

- Country X is a society based on the Confucian values of hard work, education, devotion to family, and business acumen and has exposure to European and American influences as well.

- Country X has consumers who highly value products from the United States and other Western nations. Positive identification with American brand names is extremely high.

- Country X has recently undergone a transformation from a socialist, centrally planned economy in which the private sector was declared illegal to a market economy with the most liberal foreign investment code in the region.

- Country X has been in a virtual time warp for 15 years, missing out on such developments as the information technology revolution. It has pent-up demand for infrastructure rebuilding, computers, construction, transportation, and, well, almost everything. Conveniently, it is now receiving a sizable infusion of international aid and lending to fund many of these projects.

- Country X is a nation that, despite its official ranking as one of the world's poorest societies, has thriving urban centers with a burgeoning middle class. Fueling this development are a million relatives from North America who pump an estimated $1 billion in gold and hard currency into the local economy annually through gifts to their families.

The best and brightest of this overseas community also stand ready to serve as a bridge between Country X and the West to help expand commercial relations.

- Finally, Country X is a market that for the last several years has hosted an onslaught of businesspeople from Taiwan, Hong Kong, Australia, Singapore, and France who have been learning the market and locking up deals while America has been "missing in action."

If such a country existed—and indeed it does—I think your reaction would be the same as mine: We have to be there. It's time to get moving.

Doing Business in Vietnam is designed to help you identify your potential in Vietnam and help you make your first moves into one of the world's last business frontiers.

The book is divided into two parts. The first, "The New Vietnam: Asia's Next Tiger," covers the dramatic sweep of policy changes and market conditions as well as the range of opportunities created by these developments. It also deals up front with the problems and pitfalls generic to developing markets and specific to Vietnam.

The second part, "The Doing Business in Vietnam Resource Guide," sets forth the practical information you need to begin exploring the market. Unlike Mexico, for example, where most businesspeople begin with a foundation of experience built by traveling in the country and being exposed to the culture, Vietnam is uncharted terrain for most people. The *new* Vietnam is unknown to virtually everyone. Although this book is not a travel guide, I have tried to answer your questions about *business* travel in Vietnam and offer a sense of what it's like to be there and to be operating there.

My preparation for writing this book includes ten research missions to Vietnam, interviews with dozens of businesspeople and government officials, and the study of hundreds of articles, books, pamphlets, and state documents. One conclusion that came through most clearly is that Vietnam is a land of ceaseless change. Even though only months elapsed between my visits, each time I confronted developments in policy and in everyday life that were new and unrecognizable.

This observation is meant in part to caution you that the conditions described in this book could change overnight. Change is what Vietnam is all about.

But I also mean to underscore a basic theme of *Doing Business in Vietnam*: Vietnam is an entrepreneur's paradise and *all* that this entails—the opportunities and the risks. If anyone tells you that Vietnam is the private preserve of the blue-chip giants, he or she is dead wrong. Even many big companies are starting out small. The average investment is still less than $10 million, and many projects are being undertaken with a commitment of $500,000 or less.

The willingness to take risks, to be adaptable, to improvise, to move quickly and change abruptly, to get your hands dirty, and to consider lines of business you have never considered before—these are prized qualities in Vietnam, and they make this market ideally suited for smaller companies and entrepreneurs.

This does not mean that profits will come quickly and easily or that homework and careful, detailed preparation are not necessary. The Vietnamese have a saying: *Muon canh ngot thi ham lau!* (pronounced "moon cun nok tee hum low": "If you want good-tasting soup, then boil it well!"). And so it is with doing business in the new Vietnam.

2

DOI MOI: WHAT IT MEANS TO VIETNAM, WHAT IT MEANS TO YOU

Hanoi, April 21, 1994. Just two-and-a-half months after the lifting of the trade embargo, forty-eight U.S. companies displayed products, from computers to cellular phones to snack foods, at Vietnamerica Expo '94, the first American trade show in Vietnam in decades.

Thousands of everyday Vietnamese descended on the exhibit hall to gawk at MTV, pound away on computer keyboards, and use vending machines and ATMs for the first time. Many of the younger attendees took the opportunity to practice their English on the profusely sweating Americans who were overdressed for the climate in ties and jackets.

An Embargo We Thought Would Never End

Such a scene would have been unthinkable six months earlier because of the trade embargo, which, under the terms of the Trading with the Enemy Act, made it a federal crime for an American to do business in or with Vietnam.

The embargo was imposed on communist North Vietnam in 1954 and expanded to cover the entire country following the fall of South Vietnam in 1975. Nineteen years after the end of the war and 21 years after the end of U.S. involvement in the war, the embargo remained in place. Officially, the reasons given were (1) Vietnam's failure to fully account for U.S. servicemen listed as missing in action and (2) the country's military aggression in the region, specifically, its invasion of Cambodia in 1978.

Many suspect that the true reasons for the U.S.'s remaining on a wartime footing for so long run much deeper:

1. Frustration over the U.S. defeat in Indochina and the need to "punish" the victor for winning.
2. Lack of a strong constituency for lifting the embargo in the face of pleas from veterans groups, the families of those missing in action, and elements of the Vietnamese-American community that Vietnam be ostracized and internationally isolated.
3. Another manifestation of a self-defeating attitude among many U.S. policymakers and citizens that trade is a "gift" we bestow on another country rather than a vital necessity for our own country. Should a country "misbehave," we take the gift away with little thought to the harm it could do to our own well-being.

Vietnamese officials like to portray the lengthy extension of the embargo as a one-sided punitive action by

American officials who could not bear to "swallow the bitter pill" of defeat. But it's not that simple.

After taking office in 1977, the Carter administration was reported to have opened discussions with the Vietnamese regarding normalization of relations, but the communists' stubborn demands for the payment of reparations torpedoed the talks. Reestablishing ties so soon after the debacle would have been difficult enough, but can you image any U.S. president having to explain to the American people why the taxpayers should pay the communist forces of Vietnam billions of dollars after they routed our allies in the south?

Then came the invasion of Cambodia in 1978. Although it toppled the abhorrent Khmer Rouge regime, it also installed a Vietnamese puppet government and rekindled fears in the region over the territorial aims of Vietnam, which at the time maintained the fourth largest standing army in the world.

The U.S. relationship with China was also becoming increasingly important to the United States, and it suited the Chinese fine that we continued to isolate its historical adversary. Both the United States and China also took note of how quickly Vietnam became a client state of the Soviet Union after 1975, adding to the feeling that the country was still an active enemy.

Then there were the behind-the-scenes machinations of other countries and allies in the region that didn't object too strongly to the fact that the United States was keeping its own companies away from an emerging market, leaving the field wide open for them.

I recall a meeting I attended in 1991 with a senior official in Singapore and former California Governor George Deukmejian. Earlier in the day the governor had made a speech calling for an end to the U.S. embargo and told the official about his views. The official disagreed, saying that small countries like Singapore were counting on the United States to protect them "from the aggressive tendencies of the Vietnamese." Singapore at the time was Vietnam's number one trading partner!

By 1991, conditions had changed radically. The Vietnamese had withdrawn from Cambodia, and a peace process, however tenuous, was under way. The Soviet Union was no more. The U.S. relationship with China had soured in the aftermath of the Tienamen Square massacre. Greater assistance in accounting for MIAs was forthcoming from Vietnamese authorities. And with Vietnamese-Americans now routinely permitted to return home to visit their families, the fervor in that community for perpetual isolation of their homeland lessened significantly.

In response, the Bush and Clinton administrations began a step-by-step weakening of the embargo to the point where U.S. companies could open offices, sign contracts, and hire staff. The only thing they couldn't do was make money! That all changed on February 3, 1994.

The Embargo Wasn't the Biggest Hurdle for International Business!

The grand reentry of American products to Vietnam that I and thousands of others witnessed in Hanoi at Vietnamerica Expo '94 was made possible by the embargo's end. But not too long ago the Expo would have been unthinkable for another reason as well: Vietnam was suffocating under a moribund state-owned and state-run economy that literally outlawed the private sector and rejected foreign investment.

Doi moi—remember that Vietnamese phrase (it is pronounced "doy moy"). For the businessperson looking at this market, it is the single most important phrase you could know. Literally translated it means "renovation" or "rebirth," but it has come to represent a wholesale transformation of the Vietnamese economy from a centrally planned socialist wasteland to a tumultuous market economy based on incentive, the profit motive, and the encouragement of both private enterprises and foreign investment.

Without *doi moi,* I wouldn't be writing this book. Without *doi moi,* few people would really care whether the U.S. embargo was lifted. Economically, there would be no discernible reason to take any interest in Vietnam.

FROM DISASTER TO *DOI MOI*

As summarized in an analysis prepared by Library of Congress researchers in 1989,

> Since 1975 the [Vietnamese] regime has zig-zagged through various economic changes, initially toward centralization, collectivization, eradication of private enterprise and radical social transformation. In the mid-1970s there was a precipitous campaign to dismantle the south's free enterprise economic infrastructure and integrate it with the north's centralized system.
>
> The results were disastrous, and the move further alienated the nation's most productive agricultural region. After 1978, the government oscillated between tentative economic liberalization and tighter controls, and deterioration continued.

These policy disasters, coupled with a debilitating war in Cambodia, took a ghastly toll. Whereas other countries in the region began to soar, deprivation in Vietnam triggered a mass exodus of "boat people." No one really knows how many tens, if not hundreds, of thousands of these people died at sea from starvation, dehydration, storms, sharks, and murderous pirates.

THE BIRTH OF *DOI MOI:*
FROM SMALL STEPS TO GIANT LEAPS

Most observers trace the stirring of revolutionary new policies with the Sixth Communist Party Congress in December 1986. Pressured by both the dismal failure of current policies and a new generation of leaders, the Congress took some tentative but important steps:

- Farming was decollectivized, resulting in the individual's enjoying far greater control over crops and profits.
- The concept of private industry outside the state-run sector was introduced and encouraged.
- State enterprises and individual regions (particularly in the south) were given more autonomy and discretion to respond to market conditions.
- Price controls were dismantled and state subsidies reduced.
- It was decided that foreign investment would be allowed and that Vietnam would compete regionally for foreign involvement in economic development.

A year later, in December 1987, the Law on Foreign Investment was passed, the single most important policy manifestation of *doi moi*. These measures, together with key amendments and regulations passed in 1990, 1992, and 1993, along with regular supplements, constitute the most liberal foreign investment policy in the region, permitting 100% foreign ownership of ventures and including a broad schedule of special incentives and tax holidays. (For a closer look at these measures, see chapter 15 in the Resource Guide.)

Equally as important as the laws and regulations embodying *doi moi* (which are continually evolving, usually, but not always, for the better) is a societal shift. The state-controlled mass media have ensured that *doi moi* is a household phrase and a grassroots movement. Many of the militaristic billboards adorning city neighborhoods and remote highways have been replaced by banners extolling the virtues of *doi moi* and imploring the populace to rally to its cause.

Doi moi has become the new secular religion of Vietnam. Senior ministers and cab drivers alike discuss it with ease and in positive terms, most saying it has changed life for the better.

Doi Moi in the Marketplace

Writing in the *Orange County Register* following my first visit to Vietnam in 1990, I equated Vietnamese *doi moi* with Russian *perestroika* but noted there was a key difference: "The difference is *doi moi* is working. *Perestroika* is not."

Admittedly oversimplified, my image of *perestroika* in the former Soviet Union was of shivering Muscovites waiting in long lines at the supermarket only to find that lonely, shriveled-up carrot in the vegetable bin when they finally got inside! The contrast with what I found in Saigon then could not be more striking.

(Note: readers will observe that I use both "Saigon" and the more politically correct "Ho Chi Minh City" to describe Vietnam's largest city. The latter is used when discussing the city as a political, governmental entity; the former is used to describe the city's center in geographic terms. Proper usage in different settings will be discussed fully in chapter 6.)

Walk down the streets of Saigon today or, even better, visit the home of a growing number of middle-class urban dwellers and you will see a dynamic marketplace in action:

- Color televisions and VCRs in many houses, with washing machines, microwaves, and portable telephones in some
- Amorous teenagers showing off new fashions and hairstyles on their weekly Sunday evening cruise around the city's center in which they form a parade of shiny new Honda motorbikes blocks long
- Endless rows of small family-owned storefronts with shelves and floor space stacked high with all brands of stereo equipment, big-screen TVs, and consumer goods from the world over
- Vietnamese "yuppies" in Gucci loafers walking down the street or riding in a new Toyota with one ear glued to a cellular telephone
- Sixteen cases (I'm not kidding!) of foreign beer being transported to a restaurant atop a single bicycle
- A cyclo (a three-wheeled, human-powered bicycle with a small passenger cab in front) carrying four new room air conditioners to a construction site
- Hundreds of students from children to the middle aged streaming out of after-work English language classes
- The incessant racket of jackhammers and pile drivers throughout the city, 14 hours a day, 7 days a week
- Cappuccino restaurants, pizza parlors, and bars called Hard Rock Cafe and Apocalypse Now competing side by side with sidewalk noodle shops selling *pho,* the traditional Vietnamese beef soup
- Miles of sidewalks clogged and blocked off with merchandise spilling onto the street selling the latest CDs and videotapes from America; T-shirts with slogans such as "Saigon, Vietnam," "Good Morning Vietnam," and "Lift the Embargo Now!"; books, art,

toy helicopters shaped out of discarded beer cans, and hand-carved miniature sailboats; pipes, tools, used Singer sewing machines, and porcelain bathroom fixtures; and toasters, fans, air conditioners, and copier machines

More than one observer has questioned how this level of economic activity can be sustained on the $220 per year that is purported to be the average annual income of the Vietnamese!

Of course there is a huge piece of the picture missing from my "walk" down the streets of Saigon: the 75% to 80% of the Vietnamese who live agrarian lives on the farms and the rice paddies. By almost any standard, Vietnam is a poor, underdeveloped country. Even in the more affluent cities, alongside the rapid growth you also confront beggars, orphans, and entire families living on the street with no steady means of support.

Yet, when the market is assessed from the critical standpoint of whether there are customers for you who can pay, Vietnam is following the pattern of many developing countries. Poor people scratching out subsistence-level existences represent the norm. But alongside these are millions of people with disposable incomes who are emerging into a cosmopolitan middle class bent on conspicuous consumption.

Furthermore, even poor countries have rich governments. By that I mean that, as custodians of such a large share of the national wealth as well as hundreds of millions of dollars in international aid and loans, the government itself creates many opportunities in industries such as oil and gas development, construction, engineering, architecture, and environmental control. Despite the nation's overall poverty, it does have paying customers and many projects in the pipeline.

Finally, a great deal of economic activity and wealth are masked in Vietnam because of extensive underground economic activities conducted in cash and gold. It is believed that the per capita annual income for many Saigon residents is closer to $2,000 than it is to $200, with projections that it will reach $4,000 by the year 2000.

IS *DOI MOI* HERE TO STAY?

An important consideration for any international business making a commitment in Vietnam is whether the economic reforms will be permanent. The regime dramatically changed course once. Who says that it can't happen again in a way that will threaten foreign investments?

Most observers believe there is no turning back now for Vietnam. But in the shadowy world of Vietnamese Communist Party politics, it has been reported that there are some elements not fully committed to *doi moi*.

Business News Indochina reported recently that Defense Minister Doan Khue made negative comments about the consequences of *doi moi* in the army's daily newspaper, *Quan Doi Nhan Don* (pronounced "wun doy nyung yun"): "Hostile forces are attempting to wipe out socialism and the revolutionary gains of our people. The cause of renovation...is going well and achieving many advantages, but the scheming and tricks of the enemy against our country, against socialism, remain unchanged."

Indeed, many businesspeople complain about the herky-jerky approach to policy-making and the frequent and sometimes unwelcome changes in rules and regulations. Yet few of these problems seem to be generated by any serious disputes over the wisdom of the transition to a market economy.

Pragmatism also keeps the country on course. Vietnam's fervor for the free market grew in proportion to the disintegration of its chief patron, the Soviet Union, which had been providing an estimated $1 billion a year in aid. There is no turning back because there is no one else to turn to.

Vietnamese are also a very proud, nationalistic people. (Some of their Southeast Asian neighbors will add the word *aggressive* to that description.) Many seem genuinely embarrassed that, in the era of the Pacific Rim, neighboring societies have passed them by: "Just give us time," I was told, "and we'll move ahead of many of those who today are ahead of us."

The bottom line on the survival of *doi moi*, according to Deputy Foreign Minister Le Mai, is that

> there is unanimity over turning our command economy into a market economy. We were in a very deep and serious social and economic crisis in the mid-1980s. Our mistake was we thought the market economy only applied to capitalism, not to socialism. Then we realized that whether a capitalist or socialist country . . . the law of the marketplace works.

WHAT *DOI MOI* IS NOT

It is essential to understand that although the government has loosened its grip economically and, to a degree, socially, politically Vietnam is an unrepentant one-party communist state.

Vietnam calls itself a socialist country, not a communist one, although the sole party allowed, and the central unifying force in the country, is the Vietnamese Communist Party. Labels are less important than the fact that although authorities have permitted some loosening of the reins over thought, speech, life-styles, and economic decision making, the press is not free, and dissent that challenges the supremacy of one-party rule by the Communist Party is not allowed. Vietnamese are essentially free to practice their personal religious beliefs (primarily Buddhism, Confucianism, and Catholicism), but authorities have cracked down hard when in their view organized religion crosses the line into political protest or social foment.

Some vestiges of what we associate with a communist police state have been peeled away. Although there are a limited number of political prisoners in Vietnam, the network of "reeducation camps," to which thousands of high-ranking allies of the U.S.-backed government in the south were sent, has been dismantled. Internal travel permits are no longer required. Visitors no longer have to reregister with immigration authorities 24 hours after arriving in the country. Many popular Western books and magazines are available for "unofficial" sale on the streets with no apparent effort to prevent it.

In the early days of *doi moi* (1989–90), some foreigners reported extensive spying on their business activities—principally in the form of their local office staff's being forced to give reports to local police—but I cannot confirm this. Those same sources now tell me that they believe this no longer occurs.

The Vietnamese press has even loosened to a degree, allowing exposure of extravagant or corrupt officials for their *cua chua* (public squandering) ways.

For example, an article published recently by the government-controlled English-language daily *Vietnam News* reported that "we found that many state offices are competing against each other in the acquisition of luxurious cars.... How many banquets have been thrown using public funds, how many gifts were presented to each other utilizing common assets?... The abuse of power of public officials is spreading to all fields."

We should not read too much into such self-flagellation. Authoritarian governments frequently point to permitted criticism of process, procedure, and competence as evidence of a "free" press, but in fact the press is not free in Vietnam. No debate is allowed on the basic political questions.

Still, the reporting of business news and economic developments appears open and frank. Vietnamese see themselves in the midst of a great adventure of reform, and they know the road will be bumpy. Projects gone bust are usually fully reported and analyzed to see what could be done better the next time. When a complaint is raised about the business climate, it is usually not hushed up but rather is brought out into the open, debated, and often improved on.

Although the situation is undoubtedly different for local residents, from the perspective of the foreign visitor Saigon (and increasingly Hanoi and Da Nang) doesn't have the look or feel of a police state. The climate is one of fluid, freewheeling commercialism where everyday business and family pursuits are paramount. For better and for worse, the government does not play an all-consuming role in the daily lives of the Vietnamese. There is, as in most governments, rampant favoritism, with relatives of party members or key officials receiving the choice jobs and business opportunities while those out of favor or with no special connections are held back. Out of necessity, the government has abandoned the socialist nostrum that it must at the very least provide a job and a basic level of income and social services for every citizen.

Family—not the Communist Party, the government, or the employer—remains the central defining feature of Vietnamese society.

Authorities are well aware that many advocates of Western-style democracy and human rights are winking at each other knowingly and predicting that Vietnam's effort to marry economic liberalism with political authoritarianism won't survive there any more than it did in places like South Korea, Taiwan, Thailand, and the Philippines. Sooner or later, affluent citizens will rise up and demand political rights along with their economic rights.

Such talk in the wrong places is counterproductive. Public predictions by Western politicians and business leaders that economic reform will trigger political reform only strengthen the hand of the remaining hardliners and sometimes, as the Tienamen Square massacre proved in China, with disastrous consequences.

Mo cua thi ruoi muoi va bui-bam se theo vao! (pronounced "muh kua tee roo-e moo-e vah buoy balm sek tail vow": "Open the door and the dust flies in!"). This Vietnamese proverb articulates something else the country is trying to prevent from taking root in the era of *doi moi:* the growth of a sin industry and other forms of exploitation endemic to most poor, developing nations eager to please foreign visitors and investors. One Vietnamese put it to me bluntly, saying, "We do not intend to become another Thailand."

Sexual mores are comparatively conservative in Vietnam. Prostitution exists as it exists almost everywhere. Even so, most of the young women working in bars or as paid dance partners in the clubs would take offense at the suggestion of anything untoward. Virginity until marriage (at least for women) is still considered the norm. Nightclubs and tour operators, including those with foreign investors, have been closed down by the government when suspected of catering to the sex trade or sex tours.

Vietnam was under the domination of China for approximately 1,000 years. In the second half of the twentieth century, the Vietnamese successfully fought the French, the Americans, and, briefly in 1979, the Chinese. The motivating factor behind the readiness to accept never-ending deprivation and conflict was the dream of being free from foreign domination. *Doi moi* means opening up to the world community but only while maintaining a uniquely Vietnamese politics, culture, and society. Signs of the exploitation of labor or women evoke strong negative reactions among the Vietnamese of all ideological complexions. Involvement in these activities, particu-

Doi Moi: *What It Means to Vietnam, What It Means to You* 23

larly if discovered or flaunted, can ruin your reputation in the country and only play into the hands of the hardliners, who still think it was a mistake to allow you in.

VIETNAM TODAY

Just six years into its reform experiment, Vietnam is coming on strong and fast. It went from near famine to becoming the third largest rice exporter in the world, following Thailand and the United States, and it could become number two any time! The economy grew by 7.5% in 1993 with an inflation rate of 5.1%, down from nearly 700% in 1987. It has a stable currency and a stable government.

Vietnam is rejoining the world community. Talks are under way to allow Vietnam membership in ASEAN, the Association of Southeast Asian Nations. Nearly 900 foreign investment projects involving $8.5 billion in capital have been approved. Richard Martin, the Hanoi-based general manager of the ANZ bank, reports, "In general terms, the economy is being managed well. The government has embarked upon a road of reform to which they have been quite committed and from which they are certainly not deviating." John Harvey, the executive in charge of Indochina for the "Big Six" accounting firm Ernst & Young, concludes, "Vietnam can be the next Asian tiger. The question is when?"

Let's look at where Vietnam stands today from several perspectives.

Country Profile

Official name: Socialist Republic of Vietnam
Capital: Hanoi

Official language:	Vietnamese
Population:	71 million (1994 estimate)
Population growth rate:	2.2%
Land area:	329,707 square kilometers (128,066 square miles, or slightly smaller than California)
Major cities:	Ho Chi Minh City (4.1 million population), Hanoi (2.1 million), Hai Phong (1 million), Da Nang (750,000). Major population centers are the Red River Delta in the north and the Mekong River Delta in the south.
Coastline:	2,500 kilometers (1,600 miles)
Natural resources:	Oil, natural gas, coal, minerals, agricultural land, forests, and marine resources
Life expectancy:	62.7 years
Infant mortality rate:	49 per 1,000
Adult literacy rate:	88%
Roads:	87,507 kilometers
Railways:	3,259 kilometers

Political Profile

The Communist Party of Vietnam   The April 1992 Constitution recognized the Communist Party of Vietnam as the leading force of the state and society but also stipulates that the party should operate within the framework of the country's laws.

General Secretary:	Mr. Do Muoi
Central Committee:	Approximately 145 "official members"
Estimated membership:	Approximately 2.5 million countrywide

The Central Government The National Assembly, comprised of 395 members, is elected to legislate, amend the Constitution, and elect the head of government (the prime minister) and the head of state (the president).

The prime minister (Mr. Vo Van Kiet) and his cabinet of ministers run the day-to-day affairs of the country.

The president (Mr. Le Duc Anh) serves as the head of state, with overall responsibility for the armed forces and conduct of foreign policy, and the Supreme People's Court, which oversees the nation's legal affairs and court system.

Local Government There are forty provinces, three stand-alone municipalities (Hanoi, Hai Phong, and Ho Chi Minh City), and one special zone in Uung Tau-Con Dao under the administration of the central government. Each is governed by a "people's council" that names a "people's committee" to manage local affairs and services. Thus, when you are referring to, for example, the People's Committee of Ho Chi Minh City, you are referring to Vietnam's equivalent of city hall.

Economic Profile

1993 GDP growth rate:	7.5%
GDP per capita:	$220 per year
1993 inflation:	5.1%
Workforce:	32 million
1993 jobless:	22% (estimate of urban jobless)

Wage rate:	$30 to $40 per month
Currency:	Dong (U.S.$1.00 = 10,700 dong)
Trade:	1993 exports—$3 billion
	1993 imports—$3.1 billion
Principal exports:	Crude oil, rice, marine products, coffee, coal, rubber, handicrafts, and wood products
Principal imports:	Fuel, capital equipment, vehicles, fertilizers, and consumer goods
Foreign tourists:	1993—700,000
	1991—300,000
Foreign investment:	895 projects with registered capital of $8.5 billion (from 1987, as of March 1994)
Major investors:	In order by number of projects: Hong Kong, Taiwan, South Korea, France, Japan, and Australia
	In order by amount of capital: Taiwan, Hong Kong, France, Australia, South Korea, and Japan
Major investments:	Oil and gas, manufacturing, hotels, and tourism

VIETNAM'S MIXED ECONOMY

In the West, we think of a mixed economy as one in which the private sector conducts most of the economic activity. The public sector regulates business and taxes both employers and employees to provide public services.

In Vietnam, the concept of a mixed economy is entirely different. Government not only regulates business; it also conducts business in all sectors and owns many businesses.

One of *doi moi*'s most important effects was not only the legalization of the private sector but also the unshackling of the publicly owned companies, allowing them to make their own business decisions while at the same time forcing them to compete in the marketplace with reduced subsidies.

Analysts at Price Waterhouse in Hong Kong size up the current role of the state-owned companies this way:

> In the last six years, as a result of the reform program, thousands of smaller state enterprises have had to face reality and have closed down—literally just shut their doors, in the absence of any bankruptcy laws in Vietnam—leaving the state sector leaner and more efficient than it was. Many other small enterprises, cooperatives and unions have also merged to create a greater critical mass.
>
> But the remaining 6,000–7,000 government-owned businesses still absorb a disproportionate level of the country's meager resources. According to a government economist, they still hold approximately 75% of Vietnam's assets, employ 30% of the labor force and utilize 85% of available bank credit; yet they generate only 30% of the country's GDP.

Economic planners are also toying with the concept of selling shares in public companies to private investors while maintaining a significant minority interest for the government.

As for the private sector, the Vietnam Chamber of Commerce and Industry reports that by the end of 1993 there were 4,212 private enterprises nationwide. (This total does not truly capture the extent of private business activity in Vietnam, as it does not include the millions of small family-owned retail establishments and other forms of commercial activity that individuals engage in to supplement their small salaries.)

Of the private companies, 1,796 are involved in industry, 1,804 in material supply trading, 389 in construction, 82 in housing services, 58 in transport and communication, 33 in science, 27 in agriculture, and 12 in forestry.

The average size of the private company is very small; virtually all of them employ 500 or fewer workers. These companies tend to have little operating capital, relying instead on access to land as the basis for attracting investment and credit.

Dealing in what the Vietnamese call their "multisector" economy means that your business partner and customer may be either a government-owned company or a private enterprise. Investors see advantages and disadvantages with each. State-owned enterprises may have a longer track record, more capital, greater volume, and better connections by virtue of being attached to a particular ministry. Yet many have been grossly mismanaged and are mired in bureaucracy.

Private companies tend to be more aggressive, faster moving, and infused with a more entrepreneurial spirit. Yet they can lack experience and capital, and their viability and honesty are more difficult to check. Still, many investors see opportunity in seeking out these small, struggling operations that have at least done the spadework and in teaming up with them for expansion.

Few doubt that the growth of the private sector and the privatization of the public sector is the wave of the future in Vietnam. To find out where you fit in that future, turn the page!

3

VIETNAM: A WORLD OF OPPORTUNITIES

"It's going to be a scramble here. The country's so young in its economic development, there's room for everyone in every field."

The enthusiasm embodied in that statement by an American business consultant in Vietnam may be overstated but is understandable. Spend any time in Vietnam observing and reading about the diversity of activity going on around you, and you might come to the same conclusion. Entrepreneurally minded individuals like *Vietnam Investment Review*'s Ross Dunkley see "opportunities on every street corner," which he also says can be a problem because of the temptation to do so many things that you end up doing none of them well.

Newsreel: "The Mad Scramble" in Vietnam

I have put together a short "newsreel" of recent announcements and activities to show you what I mean:

- Sixty Mercedes Benzes now sold monthly in Vietnam, forty-five to local residents
- American cotton firm signs deal to supply assembly line for processing
- John Denver to perform shows in Hanoi and Ho Chi Minh City
- Vietnam Airlines to buy thirty to forty aircraft by the year 2000
- DuPont to open Ho Chi Minh City office
- $20,000 worth of Vietnamese handicrafts sold to Texas
- McDonald's "anxious to sell" in Vietnam
- First postembargo film to be shot in Vietnam
- U.S. pharmaceutical concern licensed for joint venture
- Keppel Group of Singapore to build $6.6 million shipyard on Saigon River
- Chicago ad firm signs joint venture with Vietnamese company
- American President Lines begins full service to Vietnam
- $200 million in golf resorts now committed to Vietnam
- New York-based construction and traffic development firm to help build Ho Chi Minh City subway system
- Agriculture product processing and foodstuff industries are priorities for Vietnam

- Singer to set up production plants in Ho Chi Minh City
- Hanoi seeks firefighting and rescue equipment for new tall buildings
- Ramada plans three-star hotel in downtown Saigon
- American automakers eye expanding Vietnamese market
- Video fever hits Hanoi, karaoke craze levels off
- Northern Telecom of Canada opens Hanoi office
- Pierre Cardin brings first fashion show to Vietnam
- Big Blue forges ahead in Vietnam

Is there a role for you in this fast-paced action film? Hong Kong businessman Peter Yu, who has successfully cracked the Chinese and Korean markets, is now focusing on Vietnam. In true entrepreneurial fashion, he lets the opportunities determine his course, not simply his previous lines of business, and so is engaged in projects ranging from office complexes to golf courses to the travel business. He sums it up this way: "Vietnam has tremendous potential. The people are hardworking and smart and there is less red tape than China."

David Pang, Asia-Pacific vice president of DuPont, is high on Vietnam as well. "For DuPont," he told the *Vietnam Investment Review,* "Vietnam is going to be a big focal point, not only in terms of the growing domestic market, but also in helping us to serve the economies and markets of the entire region."

Where is your opportunity? Where is your niche? Let's survey the field from a number of perspectives.

WHERE IS THE MONEY GOING TODAY?

To begin, let's take a look at where investors who are making a commitment in Vietnam have put their money.

Who are these businesspeople, and what fields of endeavor have they chosen?

General profile of foreign investment in Vietnam

Number of projects:	895 (as of March 1994)
Total licensed capital:	$8.5 billion (as of March 1994)
Actual capital invested:	$2.08 billion
Average capital per project:	$9.9 million (73% are under $5 million)
Number of expired projects:	115 ($612 million in capital)
Value of goods generated by projects:	$780 million
Direct jobs created:	50,000
Indirect jobs created:	100,000

Foreign investment by country (number of projects)

Hong Kong	165	Taiwan	116
South Korea	55	Singapore	50
Japan	49	France	45
Australia	41	Thailand	39
Former Soviet Union	32	Malaysia	26
Russian Federation	19	China	18
Canada	16	United Kingdom	15
Germany	13	British Virgin Islands	10
Indonesia	10	Switzerland	10
Holland	9	Philippines	9
Italy	6	Sweden	6

Sectors of foreign investment in Vietnam (number of projects)

Agriculture and fishing	29
Chemicals, fertilizer, rubber production	54
Construction	15
Electrical appliances and electronics	32
Banking	4
Food industry	102
Forestry, wood products	56
Garments	50
Glassware, ceramics	8
Health services, sports	13
Hotels	108
Leather industry and production	19
Materials for construction	33
Machinery and equipment	32
Manufacture of fine arts production	8
Metal products	8
Metallurgy	6
Office rental	16
Oil exploitation and fuels	36
Paper	14
Post office and telecommunications	9
Printing	3
Textile products	25
Tourist and public services	42
Trading and supplies	4
Training and education	3
Transportation	51

Top ten locations of foreign investment projects in Vietnam (number of projects)

Ho Chi Minh City	333
Hanoi	127
Dong Nai province	52
Ba Ria-Vung Tau province	34
Khanh Hoa province	27
Quang Nam-Da Nang	25
Hai Phong	23
Soc Trang province	23
Offshore	23
Quang Ninh province	13

THE "OFFICIAL" PRIORITIES: WHAT THE VIETNAMESE GOVERNMENT WANTS

In its official pronouncements on economic development priorities, the Vietnamese government says all the things you would expect any government in a developing country to say: We want manufacturing investment, we want tourism, and we want high technology.

Still, the government's priorities are worth paying attention to. After all, the same government decides whether you will be allowed to conduct business in Vietnam, grants special tax and other incentives to favored projects, and even joins as an official partner with foreign companies.

Many times your business partner in Vietnam *is* the government—either a ministry of the central government, a local people's committee, or a state- or city-owned company under its purview. Although there are many opportunities available in areas the authorities have chosen not to emphasize, it can't hurt if there is a nexus between the kind of business you are in or want to be in and the kind of business the Vietnamese government is most anxious to have.

What are the government's priorities?

In the broadest sense, the Law on Foreign Investment (see chapter 15 in the Resource Guide) sets forth those categories that are to be given priority by the government through its approval process, its utilization of precious hard currency, and the incentives that are granted to the investor. The areas are as follows:

- Infrastructure projects
- Those producing goods for export
- Those producing goods that substitute for imports
- Those involving the transfer of high technology
- Large projects, defined as those with capitalization in excess of $10 million
- Labor-intensive manufacturing
- Tourism

In addition, specific projects needing foreign investment and involvement are devised and developed by the State Committee for Cooperation and Investment (SCCI) in concert with appropriate ministries and regions throughout the country. (The SCCI is the one-stop government agency responsible for both promoting foreign investment in Vietnam and licensing virtually all foreign business ventures. I will discuss the all-important role of the SCCI in the next chapter.)

You can get the current "List of Projects Under Promotion" by contacting the SCCI (to find out how, see chapter 13 in the Resource Guide). Should you want to know more about a certain project, the SCCI can provide a detailed profile. In some cases the projects involve establishing an entirely new facility, whereas others entail upgrading an existing operation. Here are a few wide-ranging examples from the SCCI's June 1993 list of 200 projects under promotion:

- Cashew nut processing in Dong Nai province; total investment $4.2 million
- Canned fruit for export in Tuyen Quang province; total investment $2.5 million
- Tea bag production in Hanoi; total investment $1.6 million
- Production of bamboo and rattan for export in Vinh Phu province; total investment $1.3 million
- Mineral water exploitation in Hai Hung province; total investment $1.1 million
- Sand mining and glass manufacturing in Quang Binh province; total investment $4.6 million
- Gemstone mining and processing in Binh Thuan province; total investment $430,000
- Modernization of pharmaceutical industry in Ho Chi Minh City; total investment $3.9 million
- Agriculture machine assembling and manufacturing in Ho Chi Minh City; total investment $900,000
- Diesel engine production in Hanoi; total investment $19 million
- Sports shoes and working gloves facility in Hanoi; total investment $2.1 million
- High-grade furniture manufacturing in Binh Thuan province; total investment $2.7 million
- Expansion of Cuu Long rice mill in Tra Vinh province; total investment $2.0 million
- Expansion of Can Tho Port in Can Tho Province; total investment $11.1 million
- Upgrading of Highway 1 (the North-South Highway); total investment $100 million and up for each major segment

Special Note: Tapping into International Lending and Aid

After years of being denied such international assistance, Vietnam is counting on grants and loans from the World Bank, the International Monetary Fund, and the Asian Development Bank to fund its most important infrastructure projects.

The money is starting to flow. At a donor conference in Paris in late 1993, for example, Vietnam racked up $1.86 billion. The World Bank has agreed to loan $270.5 million specifically for upgrading major sections of Highway 1, which is the key north-south link stretching from Saigon to Hanoi.

Vietnam is a country that needs almost everything but can pay for very little. These projects are attracting many eager bidders not only because they represent important international business but because companies can see clearly that there is a mechanism for getting paid.

Naturally, the world's premier construction and engineering firms are eagerly getting in on the action, but even smaller firms in fields such as engineering, architecture, pollution-control technology, law, financial consulting, and many others related to major multifaceted projects should take steps to contact the international financing institutions to establish a foundation for bidding on contracts and subcontracts. You may contact the following groups:

Asian Development Bank
6 ADB Avenue, Mandaluyoung
Metro Manila, Philippines
Tel: 63-2-711-3851

International Monetary Fund
700 19th Street N.W.
Washington, D.C. 20431
Tel: 202-623-7000

World Bank
1818 H Street N.W.
Washington, D.C. 20433
Tel: 202-473-1964
Fax: 202-676-0635

OPPORTUNITIES BY REGION

Despite political reunification in 1975, Vietnam is still a country of distinct regions. Most notable in the consciousness of the Vietnamese is the distinction between north and south. Despite the fact that 87% of the Vietnamese people spring from the same ethnic heritage (Kinh), accents, attitudes, and patterns of history and economic development differ from region to region.

Vietnamese often compare their country to a bamboo pole carried over the shoulder with a rice basket on each end. Each rice basket represents a major farm-to-market population center. In the south, Ho Chi Minh City sits on the northern rim of its rice and seafood bowl, the Mekong Delta. Nearby are the major ports of Saigon and Vung Tau.

In the north are Hanoi and the Red River Delta, connected (tenuously) to the outside world by the ports of Hai Phong and Hon Gai. Each "rice basket" is very densely populated. The north carries the weight politically and governmentally and the south commercially.

The long, slender section of the country connecting the northern and southern powerhouses is, relatively speaking, sparsely populated, with the exception of a bulge in the center that constitutes the Da Nang area. Yet, what it lacks in human resources it makes up for in natural ones such as forests, minerals, and scenic beauty, particularly along the shore, which is ideal for the development of tourism.

Vietnamese officials are well aware of the problems that have plagued other emerging markets as a result of the uneven pace of economic development. Not only does this create regional tensions and potential political instability, but, as can be seen in the Philippines and Thailand, economic inequality spawns mass migration of the populace to the urban centers, bringing with it a host of social problems.

But being aware of the problem doesn't mean it will go away. The pace of economic development is indeed uneven. By a variety of indicators, Ho Chi Minh City is "ahead" of Hanoi, and both cities are ahead of outlying population centers.

The government has and will continue to try to balance the scales through various policies. It actively promotes, through its list of projects under promotion, businesses that will bring resource development and jobs to outlying areas. It will also "spread the wealth" when it comes to allocating infrastructure dollars and special tax and regulatory incentives.

The nature of your business will play a major role in determining which region or regions you should focus on. For example, if you are exploring opportunities in agriculture and related fields, you will be spending a great deal of time in the Mekong Delta. The Da Nang area of central Vietnam will be of little interest for the foreseeable future. Yet if you hail from the tourist industry, Da Nang will be a high priority; the Mekong Delta won't be.

As you make your initial, exploratory visit to Vietnam, you will quickly be able to determine which parts of the country you need to focus on. Inevitably, however, for one purpose or another, you will gravitate to the north or the south and use Hanoi or Ho Chi Minh City as your base, fanning out from there if necessary. Because the government promotes investments in areas where there is little business, you may also be wise to look for a foundation in an area that is not so highly developed.

Ho Chi Minh City and the South

As a rule, foreign businesspeople are most comfortable operating out of Ho Chi Minh City. The region has a strong commercial and entrepreneurial tradition and has been heavily influenced, despite 20 years under communism, by its previous experiences with the French, Americans, and ethnic Chinese. Less isolated than Hanoi, it burst out of the starting gate on the inception of *doi moi* and has been building on its own momentum ever since.

The city accounts for an estimated one-fifth of the country's gross domestic product, one-third of the industrial output, 70% of the foreign trade, and approximately 41% of the foreign investment.

The infrastructure, level of training, and per capita income of the south surpass those of other regions. There is rich agricultural land, offshore oil, extensive marine resources, and an abundant supply of labor. A shortage of power causes frequent but usually brief blackouts that disrupt business operations; however, a new transmission line is being opened to assist in transferring power from the North to the South.

Mr. Tran Thien Tu, vice chairman of Ho Chi Minh City's office in charge of promoting and signing off on foreign investment, told me that infrastructure projects and manufacturing facilities are the city's highest priorities. Plans are in the works to expand the city across the Saigon River; build a subway system, bridges, and a tunnel under the river that will include access for bicycles; and construct facilities ranging from a cement plant to a major supermarket.

"There are opportunities for smaller investors as well," Mr. Tu confirmed. "Most of the activity to date has been of this nature, so obviously we approve of it." He adds that the Ho Chi Minh City government is ready to help foreign companies, large and small, find a partner and a location.

Hanoi and the North

The northern region is rich in natural resources such as coal, iron, kaolin, limestone, and forest products and thus offers major potential for heavy industry and mining. There is a surplus of power and an abundance of cheap labor, both of which attract manufacturers.

Hanoi is the political center of the nation and a commercial center in its own right. Approximately two hours away is the third largest city in Vietnam, the port city of Hai Phong. Major industries here include shipbuilding, machinery, and fishing.

The pace of activity in Hanoi has picked up in recent months. Hanoi People's Committee Chairman Le At Hoi predicts that $2 billion in foreign investment will be committed in 1994–95 and says that his government particularly wants to promote the development of hotels, offices, and trading service centers in the downtown area.

Even the infamous "Hanoi Hilton" is falling victim to the construction boom. The last prisoners have been removed from what Vietnamese know as the Hoa Lo prison to make way for the construction of a twenty-two-story hotel and office tower. (No, it will not be a Hilton hotel!)

Da Nang and the Central Region

With a flood of companies streaming into Hanoi and Ho Chi Minh City, many businesspeople are starting to look at the coastal city of Da Nang. A one-hour flight from either the north or the south, Da Nang is the gateway to economic development in central Vietnam as well as a potential transitway for trade with inland markets of Southeast Asia such as Laos, Cambodia, and eastern Thailand.

Da Nang is highly rated for its tourism potential, given the beautiful beaches in the area (including China

Beach) and its proximity to the historical sites of Hue. A number of hotel and tourist services projects are in the works, attracting investors from Japan, Hong Kong, Germany, and Taipei.

Despite its location and resources, Da Nang is viewed as several years behind Ho Chi Minh City and Hanoi in establishing a business climate that is user-friendly for foreign companies. Explains one leading Vietnamese businessman in Da Nang, "Under the country's new direction toward a free-market economy, we have been among the last to embark on this path. However, many of us here truly believe that in time, we'll eventually come out ahead because of Da Nang's many great natural advantages—and its destiny."

Opportunities Sector by Sector

Infrastructure

Vietnam's transportation network is dilapidated and inadequate for current needs, much less future economic growth. Roads need to be repaired and widened, bridges rebuilt, rail lines upgraded, and both seaports and airports expanded.

In addition, top priorities are improving water supply systems and building waste treatment facilities. There are many opportunities to provide technical support for these and other projects, and, as has been mentioned, funding to pay for these projects is now coming through the pipeline of international financial institutions.

A number of U.S. companies are moving fast. Fluor has established offices in Hanoi and Ho Chi Minh City to pursue work on major construction and engineering projects.

Parsons Brincherhoff, the New York–based construction and traffic development group, has signed a memorandum of understanding with the Ho Chi Minh

City government to study the feasibility of building a subway system serving the metropolitan area.

Ten American companies have entered the bidding competition for work on the reconstruction of major portions of the main north-south artery, Highway 1.

Given the priority the government has placed on infrastructure, the presence of international funding, and the breadth of services required to complete the projects, this arena offers many opportunities for participation by companies large and small.

Construction Materials and Equipment

Mr. Le Nghia Vu, director of the Ministry of Construction's Materials Trading and Building Materials Import-Export Company, told me that Vietnam needs to import ceramics, sanitary systems, tile, and other building materials. Although imports now come from Spain and Thailand, he said that "the high quality of American products in this area will be attractive to Vietnam."

Equipment for mining and earth moving is also needed. Again, Mr. Vu emphasized that although most such equipment comes from Japan, Vietnam considers American products the best.

Caterpillar has already taken steps to capitalize on this reputation. Company officials figure that Vietnam will need at least $350 million in earth-moving equipment over the next few years.

Opportunities also exist for those wanting to establish manufacturing plants for building materials and supplies. A joint venture involving an American firm is already under way in Song Be province (just north of Ho Chi Minh City along the Cambodian border) to produce high-quality construction materials.

The Ministry of Construction also identifies the production of glass and sanitation ware, as well as new technology for cement production, as its priority and will help formulate joint ventures to accomplish these goals.

Considering the fact that Vietnam essentially needs to be rebuilt from the ground up, it is not too hard to envision the scope of needs in this sector.

Manufacturing

Seeking to take advantage of wage rates between $30 and $40 per month, many international companies see Vietnam as an ideal place to establish small, medium, or large manufacturing facilities. The wage rates, however, are technically higher in Ho Chi Minh City, where a wage rate of $50 per month is commonly found in joint venture projects.

Labor-intensive, low-skilled production facilities making ceramics, building materials, and packaging (such as cardboard boxes and plastic bags) have already been opened by foreign investors.

Textile production is a prime area of opportunity, as the Ministry of Light Industry has said that it wants to encourage the establishment of at least fifteen new textile mills in the country.

A major U.S. company, Singer, has already announced major plans for Vietnam, including setting up a plant in Ho Chi Minh City to make sewing machines and other household products.

It is important to note that, in opening manufacturing facilities or starting other projects involving the need for physical plants, many investors don't start from scratch. They have determined that a good approach is to locate an existing facility to upgrade or convert.

A Hong Kong manufacturer told me that a number of relatively small investments, even in the range of $500,000, are feasible in terms of helping to establish a new production line in concert with Vietnamese partners. He also told me that those engaged in manufacturing in Vietnam are highly complimentary of their Vietnamese partners and the quality of the workers. Thomas Schwarz, a partner at Skadden, Arps, Slate, Meagher & Flom, comments that the work force in Vietnam is particularly well trained in sciences and engineering. Many Vietnamese were trained in Eastern Europe and even in Sweden.

Hotels and Tourism

In 1993, 700,000 foreign visitors arrived in Vietnam compared to just 300,000 in 1991. These tourists produced an 80% increase in revenues in just one year. The projections for the industry are for continued substantial growth.

Although Saigon has seen a frenzy of hotel construction, that city, and especially Hanoi, still fall far short of the number of international-standard rooms they need to meet the growth in international tourism. Therefore, many opportunities still exist for hotel construction, although the government is now limiting licenses to larger projects with a certain level of capital. Ramada has recently jumped into the fray with plans to build a 388-room, 20-story hotel in the center of Saigon.

On the other hand, Eugene Matthews, president of Ashta International, Inc., thinks that the real estate sector in both Hanoi and Ho Chi Minh City is over-prescribed. Numerous hotel and office projects are already underway. There is still opportunity in the central part of the country, but the infrastructure there cannot yet support large numbers of tourists.

But hotel construction is only the tip of the iceberg. There is a need for tourist facilities such as golf courses and other sporting and entertainment opportunities. Services will be needed outside Vietnam in the travel marketing business to help feed tourists into Vietnam.

Foreign tourists, many of whom are not accustomed to "roughing" it in a developing country, bring their need for comfort with them. There will be an attractive market niche for services and products directed to the exploding population of tourists, businesspeople, and resident expatriates.

Airlines, Airports, and Airplanes

Consider the following:

- Vietnam Airlines plans to replace fifteen aircraft and then double its fleet in six years.
- $2.5 billion will be spent by the year 2000 to upgrade airports in Ho Chi Minh City, Hanoi, Da Nang, Dalat, and elsewhere to handle an anticipated increase in passengers in the next few years.
- An estimated 200,000 overseas Vietnamese visited their homeland last year, most of them coming from California, Texas, and Washington, D.C., but arriving in Vietnam on Cathay Pacific, Thai, Singapore, Philippine, or Malaysian airlines!
- The airlines and aviation industries need reservation systems, marketing, air traffic control technology, jetways, maintenance, baggage-handling systems—you name it.

No wonder that Delta, United, Continental, and Northwest airlines have already come to Vietnam, with some announcing the start of service as soon as government approval is received. Boeing has been heavily involved in the market as well.

Overseas Vietnamese should take special note of the role they might play in the service and marketing ends of the airline and travel industry, given their special knowledge of the language and culture of both their new and their old country.

Computers and Information Technology

In Vietnam, there are now only three computers for every 10,000 people; by comparison, in Indonesia there are three for every 1,000 people. The potential for those involved in the fields of hardware, software, and information systems training is enormous.

The Vietnamese government plans to spend $500 million by the year 2000 to develop computer markets, with $135 million from international donors already earmarked for information technology projects.

The government is also considering Oracle software to modernize data bases at various ministries. Unisys, IBM, Digital, and Fujitsu have all been asked to develop master plans for the information technology market. IBM has reportedly signed two deals in Vietnam and is considering a local hardware manufacturing facility in the country.

Telecommunications

Along with information technology, communications technology is a major priority and is rightly considered part of its infrastruc-ture development. According to Kathleen Charlton of Ashta International, "Although opportunities in this sector are great, the competition among foreign firms is already heated."

Alcatel, a French telecommunications firm, has already signed a memorandum of understanding to invest $500 million to expand Vietnam's phone system and cellular phone network.

Motorola has opened an office in Vietnam and, according to a spokesman, identifies these key opportunities: communications infrastructure, cellular phone systems, pagers, semiconductor manufacturing, and development of rural telephone systems.

Other telecommunications companies that have played an active role in Vietnam include Telstra of Australia, Siemens of Germany, and Schlumberger of France.

Motor Vehicles and Automotive Parts

In a country of some 71.8 million people, there are currently only 250,000 four-wheeled vehicles. Although private ownership of cars will be out of reach of most Vietnamese for years to come, the need for motor vehicles, parts, and services is growing rapidly.

Vietnamese planners figure that by the year 2000 the country will need to purchase between 12,800 and 17,300 tourist cars and 47,000 to 63,000 commercial vehicles.

Thanks to joint ventures with foreign firms, Vietnam has three assembly plants of its own with a total annual capacity of 50,000 vehicles. Each of Detroit's "Big Three" automakers has been to Vietnam to evaluate the market. The verdict? Vietnam is one of the few virtually untapped markets for motor vehicles and parts.

Agribusiness

Agriculture officials in Vietnam have made it clear that they have identified and are carving out a range of opportunities for U.S. agribusiness in their country.

The opportunities emphasized by the Ministry of Agriculture and Food Industries include the following:

- Wheat milling and processing technology
- Processing products from corn
- Developing and processing rubber
- Milk production and milk cow breeding
- Pig breeding and pork processing
- Importation of insecticides and veterinary medicine

In addition, Vietnam needs to import 400,000 tons of wheat annually, anticipated to grow to 600,000 tons by the year 2000. A number of corn and soybean strains are needed, as are 200,000 tons of fertilizer per year. Food processing is also considered a high priority. The American investment and consulting company Ashta International recently signed an agreement with the National Dairy Company to establish an $18 million joint venture in dairy farming and milk processing.

Consumer Products

To capitalize on residual brand-name recognition of many American products in Vietnam, as well as on rising incomes, a number of companies have begun to move into the market.

Coca-Cola and Pepsi are two well-known examples. Phillip Morris is reportedly looking at the possibility of producing Marlboro cigarettes as well as yogurt in Vietnam for the local market. CPC International, the giant American food group, has opened an office and is looking at plans to manufacture and sell Skippy, Hellmann's, and Mazola products. Similarly, Kodak has opened a representative office and shops in Vietnam.

Fast-food restaurants such as McDonald's, KFC, and Pizza Hut have performed very well in most other Asian markets and are now laying the groundwork in Vietnam, while Dunkin' Donuts is already established there.

Entertainment, Sports, and Leisure Activities

There isn't much for young Vietnamese with rising incomes and some leisure time to do in Vietnam. Sports and recreational opportunities are scarce, as are movie theaters and concerts.

In early 1994, pop star Bryan Adams became the first westerner of note to perform in Vietnam in years, and the concert was a major event. Twenty-five hundred people paid $20 to $35 a ticket, which for many is nearly a month's salary.

A Hong Kong–based company called Sport Asia sponsored the event and plans to sponsor additional concerts as well as golf and tennis tournaments. There is certainly room for additional companies to bring more entertainment and other recreational options to the Vietnamese.

Oil and Other Natural Resources

One estimate places Vietnam's oil reserves at 1.5 to 3 billion barrels. Over two dozen foreign companies have been involved in oil exploration and exploitation since the 1980s.

In late 1993, Vietnam granted the last prime block on its southern continental shelf to Mobil, which will explore the so-called Blue Dragon field as part of a joint venture with Japanese and Indonesian involvement.

All industries related to the development of oil and gas resources—including the construction of pipelines, onshore facilities, and most especially pollution-control and cleanup technology—should look closely at Vietnam for opportunities.

Mining, timber, and the marine-products industries should also take advantage of Vietnam's substantial untapped resources.

Services

Service industries, including smaller companies and even individual professionals, should watch the maturation of the Vietnamese market closely. As the country develops, there will be an increasing need for a broad range of professional services and other functions that facilitate business. Following are some examples.

Advertising Three years ago, advertising was all but forbidden in Vietnam. Now, although in a state of flux, it is booming. There are only fifteen advertising companies in the country, and although the Vietnamese who are involved are considered to have good ideas, they lack international-standard skills. In the words of a Dutch businessman operating in Vietnam. "If international ad agencies set up offices in Vietnam, it would be a gold mine for them."

Urban Management and Planning Ministry of Construction officials told me that they consider U.S. professionals in this field the best and would welcome their involvement as Vietnam's cities engage in hectic growth and nonstop construction.

Insurance Foreign insurance companies are allowed to operate in Vietnam and can offer life, health, accident, travel, fire, shipping, aviation, and liability insurance.

Legal Services Foreign lawyers in Vietnam are not licensed as Vietnamese lawyers but can represent a broad range of client interests in the country. Although foreign law firms are still limited to having a representative office and performing advisory work, in reality, they offer various legal services.

Banking Since 1990, twenty-eight foreign banks have applied to operate in Vietnam, most as representative offices rather than branches. Bank of America was the first U.S. bank to open an office in Vietnam and is now in the process of establishing permanent branches, as is Citibank. Bank of America officials view Vietnam as a market of "high potential" for banking and financial services. According to Thomas Schwarz, "One of the most important thinks the Vietnamese government can do is to continue liberalizing its banking system and gain the confidence in the banks of the people and the local business."

Other Services

Opportunities are also emerging for those who can provide accounting services, employee and management training, public and government relations, marketing services, printing and editorial services, and consulting.

One Hong Kong businessman told me that he currently has three projects in Vietnam: a hotel, a garment factory, and a pig farm! The diversity of that one entrepreneur's portfolio characterizes the Vietnamese market today. Vietnam offers a world of opportunities for businesspeople who have the creativity and the perseverance to find their niches.

4

HOW TO DO BUSINESS IN VIETNAM: A STEP-BY-STEP PLAN

In the last chapter, we looked at business opportunities in various regions and economic sectors in Vietnam. The purpose of this chapter is to detail the strategies you should employ to seize those opportunities.

Given the short time that Vietnam has been open to foreign investment, any example of a project that is operating in the black is worth looking at closely. In 1989, several Australian entrepreneurs with both journalistic and business backgrounds packed up their families and moved to Vietnam to embark on an audacious task: to produce locally and distribute globally an English-language international business newspaper in a country where there was little international business being conducted and virtually no freedom of the press.

Joined later by several English and European investors, the group's vision was to meet what they anticipated would be a tremendous demand for business news about Vietnam as the country emerged from isolation. Their product: the *Vietnam Investment Review*.

They chose a Vietnamese partner well, selecting the State Committee for Cooperation and Investment, the very entity empowered to promote and license theirs and all other foreign investments. The committee wanted a showcase newspaper that would communicate developments to the international community.

They began the process of securing a business cooperation agreement and setting up the newspaper in 1989. By 1991 they were ready to publish, and they did so for exactly three issues before being shut down by the government!

The problem was not content but the fact that the paper was being published in Ho Chi Minh City instead of Hanoi. It seems that the government had second thoughts about allowing a newspaper produced by foreigners to be printed and distributed so far from the orbit of the national capital.

"We learned the importance of paying great deference to the fact that Ho Chi Minh City may be the commercial center of the country, but the political power is in Hanoi," says David Bagnall, one of the investors. "Initially the paper was headquartered in Ho Chi Minh. They wanted it in Hanoi. The headquarters were moved and we were back in business."

Looking back on the experience, the paper's Hanoi-based editor, Ross Dunkley, reflects:

> We made a lot of mistakes, but we were traveling in uncharted territory. For one thing we started out with less capital than we actually needed, although we didn't know it at first! It was also extremely difficult to operate in the early days. Imagine being in the newspaper business and having to spend two hours at your desk in Hanoi dialing up your reporters in Ho Chi Minh City over and over again because the call won't go through!

We also learned a lesson that still operates today. Get your foot in the door first. That is the most important step. Then deal with the rest as it comes along.

Today, the *Vietnam Investment Review* is a firmly established institution in both business and government circles. It lands on the desk of every senior government official as well as every foreign company operating in Vietnam. It frequently sells out of its weekly printing of 10,000 and has seen advertising grow by 86% in 1993 over 1992 and by 100% in 1994 over 1993. Several of the investors, including Bagnall, have sold their interest, realizing a substantial return on their original money after three years.

What lessons were learned according to the team at *Vietnam Investment Review?* Start modestly, pick a good partner, be flexible, get the best deal you can up front in negotiations with your partners and the government, but don't be concerned if you don't immediately get *everything* you want.

THE FIRST STEPS: HOW TO GET STARTED

To determine whether there is a niche for you in Vietnam, proceed the way you would before making any important business decision, that is, by doing your homework.

After reading this book, use the Resource Guide to identify publications and organizations pertinent to your endeavor as the first stage of a thorough effort to research the market.

Go to Vietnam, too! Spend some time observing and learning. Meet key government and business leaders, everyday Vietnamese, and foreign businesspeople who have already set up shop there.

One of the rewarding aspects of exploring Vietnam is that people are willing to share information and ideas as well as compare experiences. Although competition is keen and will grow only more intense in the years to come, for now there is a "we're all in this together" attitude on the part of many foreign pioneers. It is easy to fall into conversations regarding business conditions and opportunities. Individuals you meet in hotel lobbies and coffee shops will be as curious to know why you are there as you are to know why they are there. Inquiries from Vietnamese about where you come from and your goals in their country also generate friendly, educational conversations.

To begin taking these exploratory first steps, what is the best approach?

You can begin by putting together your own study mission. Set up as many meetings in advance through faxes and phone calls, but be prepared to be flexible with your schedule until you arrive. Note that very rarely will people in Vietnam return your fax due to the prohibitive cost, so be as specific as possible in your faxed requests. Also note that when you call, it is prudent to have a Vietnamese translator available. Contact the State Committee for Cooperation and Investment, the Vietnam Chamber of Commerce and Industry, the local people's committee, and the ministry related to your line of business. Set up introductory, "no commitment" meetings with one or more of the investment service companies or private consultants. By starting with this core set of meetings, you will inevitably cull from them other leads and contacts for additional appointments. If access to a translator is available, documents should be translated to make meetings more productive.

I recommend this approach for (1) companies with recognizable names, for the names themselves open doors; (2) those willing to be flexible and those who want a less structured opportunity to look around and get a feel for the market; (3) those with a fairly specific idea or easily defined business activity, making it easy to discern the people and agencies they should see; and (4) those who are intrigued by Vietnam but have absolutely no idea whether it is right for them and thus want to keep expenses and commitments to a minimum.

Don't be discouraged if the Vietnamese you contact don't fall all over themselves because you have decided to "bless them" with your presence. The Vietnam Chamber of Commerce and Industry, for example, received 9,600 foreign business visitors and delegations from fifty-two countries in 1993 alone!

Although virtually all my contacts have been friendly, open, and polite, I'm not alone in noticing a growing attitude of cockiness among Vietnamese officials as greater numbers of foreign businesspeople come knocking on their doors. You are the suitor and they the sought-after, not the other way around.

Despite genuine enthusiasm for *doi moi* and foreign investment, Vietnamese maintain a strong sense of pride. Accurate or not, the prevalent feeling is that there is a uniquely Vietnamese way of doing things, that it is the best way, and that, if they had to, they could do it alone.

A case in point is the Vietnamese government's restrained reaction to the lifting of the U.S. trade embargo. The attitude of many American policymakers seems to be that the right to trade with the United States is a generous gift bestowed on others rather than a necessity for our own prosperity. When the embargo was lifted, it was clear that, at least officially, the Vietnamese did not view it as a gift but as the cessation of an injustice. In a meeting shortly after the lifting of the embargo, the head of the America Department at the Vietnamese Ministry of Foreign Affairs went to great lengths to portray it to me as a necessary step for *America* and that the United States should expect no special business favors as a result.

Where should you begin when taking those first steps into the market, Hanoi or Ho Chi Minh City? Visit both if at all possible, but if you must choose, choose Ho Chi Minh City.

You can't do business in Vietnam without the government, and the government power is in Hanoi. But you can't understand the market without going to the marketplace, and the heart of the marketplace is in Ho Chi Minh City. Understanding should come first in these early stages.

Many companies with existing operations in Asia, particularly Southeast Asia, use those bases as launching pads for Vietnam. Since the lifting of the trade embargo, many U.S. multinational companies have assigned their Hong Kong, Singapore, or Bangkok headquarters to set up operations in Vietnam. A result is that these locales have in themselves become repositories of information, leads, contacts, and service providers related to the Vietnamese market. When conducting the research specific to this book, for example, I spent at least as much time in Hong Kong as I did in Vietnam.

Why reinvent the wheel? If you have operations in the region, have done business there before, or have existing networks of contacts in these places, tap into them and apply as much as you can to Vietnam.

Others may prefer to begin by utilizing a service company or consultant who can put an introductory study mission together for you at relatively low cost. You can end the relationship right there or continue to engage their services to assist you in finding a partner and securing a business license.

Outfits such as the Foreign Investment Service Company (FISC) or the Vietnam Chamber of Commerce and Industry's Trade Service Company can arrange an entire program for you, including securing a visa, ground arrangements, and appointments.

I have used FISC in the past and have found it inexpensive and worthwhile. For example, I once had FISC arrange a full day of meetings in Hanoi at a cost of $50, including the services of a translator!

Another option is to join one of the trade missions now being organized by groups such as state and local chambers, the American Chamber of Commerce in Hong Kong, People to People International, and the like.

Finally, you can engage the services of consultants, lawyers, or accounting firms based in the United States, Hong Kong, or Vietnam.

Even big companies such as American Express have found that working with small consulting firms is the way to go in the early stages. But remember that consultants are relatively new at this game, too, because the market itself is new. Check references of existing or previous clients as best you can before proceeding.

Chapter 12 in the Resource Guide lists many of the organizations you can contact to pursue these options. For a sample itinerary of an exploratory business mission, see chapter 11. Be sure to make the most of your trip by reading as much as you can about the people, culture, and economy before you go; but bring an extra briefcase, for many of the key documents and resources can be found only in Vietnam itself! (For more information *about* information, see chapter 14 in the Resource Guide.)

THE NEXT STEP: OPENING A REPRESENTATIVE OFFICE

Unlike the other methods of establishing a business presence in Vietnam, applications for a representative office are submitted to the Ministry of Trade and Tourism. This is because the representative office is not considered an investment.

A representative office is established to introduce a company presence in Vietnam as well as to develop contracts, customers, and investment opportunities for the parent company. However, it cannot directly engage in the buying and selling of goods and services.

Many companies find the representative office to be the best way to gain their footing in Vietnam. It is often the step that serious companies take between their initial research and market evaluation and actually making an investment or signing a business contract. By the end of 1993, 765 such offices had been licensed to open in Vietnam.

A representative office signals your commitment to the Vietnamese market and serves to establish a visible presence. Effective offices become launching pads for the development of business contracts, joint ventures, marketing plans for products, and other activities. Those providing professional services, such as lawyers and consultants, go this route as well—and that is permissible as long as they have a headquarters outside the country that conducts all the actual contracts and financial transactions with clients.

Establishing a representative office is not cheap, particularly for a smaller firm. The application fee payable to the Ministry of Trade is $5,000. A branch office costs an additional $3,000. Office space is scarce and expensive, which is why some representatives of foreign companies live and work out of hotels or guest houses until, primarily through word of mouth, they identify suitable space. Estimates for offices range from $25 to $60 per square meter.

Ministry of Trade officials told me that they are happy to "hand-hold" applicants through the process, advising them each step of the way to maximize their chances of being approved.

Two sets of application forms are required in English and Vietnamese. One set will be sent to the local government jurisdiction where the office is to be set up. Required supporting documents include a profile of the company, a bank statement, articles of incorporation, and letters of introduction and reference from Vietnamese agencies.

Ideally, the ministry will give you its answer within sixty days. If you are approved, your permission to run the office is good for three years.

One important consideration of protocol facing companies is where to establish offices: Hanoi or Ho Chi Minh City?

Remember the lesson that the *Vietnam Investment Review* learned about paying due deference to Hanoi. Major "name" corporations that plan a national strategy in Vietnam are advised to establish the main representative office in Hanoi and a branch in Ho Chi Minh City. Firms that want or can afford only one office and that need to have extensive dealings with the central government should also select Hanoi.

Smaller companies whose representative office work program is more focused on marketing and the development of commercial relations with Vietnamese companies can safely choose to locate in Ho Chi Minh City.

GOING FURTHER: FIVE APPROACHES TO DOING BUSINESS IN VIETNAM

The Vietnamese government has established five general approaches to doing business in Vietnam (importing and exporting are discussed separately in the next chapter):

1. Business cooperation contract
2. Joint venture enterprise

3. 100% foreign-owned enterprise
4. Build-operate-transfer (B.O.T.) project
5. Export processing zones

All legal forms of business activity in Vietnam entail petitioning the central, and usually the provincial or city, government for approval. Licenses to operate under the first four approaches are issued by SCCI.

For the international businessperson hoping to crack the Vietnamese market, the SCCI is the "Big Daddy" of the government. A cabinet-level agency of the central government, it was formed to be both a regulator and a promoter of foreign investment.

Developing an understanding of and contacts with the SCCI is vital from the standpoint of not only getting approved but of getting approved under the most favorable terms. The SCCI may want to engage in dialogue with you about the amount of capital you are pledging and the value being prescribed to each business partner's nonliquid capital, such as land rights. You will want to persuade the SCCI that your project qualifies for reduced or deferred taxation. Eugene Matthews suggests that companies also familiarize themselves and their projects with relevant ministries and agencies to gain approval in advance. "As part of the formal approval process, SCCI will consult with these other entities, all of whom must sign off before SCCI grants the license."

Let's briefly outline each of the business approaches established in Vietnam's Law on Foreign Investment and subsequent amendments and additions to that law.

(Note: When you want to make a more detailed study of the investment options and the application process, see chapters 15 and 16 in the Resource Guide. For specific examples of each method of business operation, see chapter 17.)

Business Cooperation Contract

The business cooperation contract is an agreement between a foreign investor and a Vietnamese partner to conduct a business operation without creating a new legal entity. A contract is developed that spells out the scope of the business to be engaged in, responsibilities and rights of each party, the equipment and materials required, the duration of the venture, and the agreed-on method of resolving disputes.

Along with the application, the business cooperation contract, feasibility study, and background information on the companies involved must be submitted.

Of the foreign projects licensed for approval so far, approximately 11% have taken the form of a business cooperation agreement, including some of the major offshore oil exploration projects.

Advantages This focused approach to doing business entails fewer legal and other entanglements than do other forms of business.

Disadvantages Contracts are hard to enforce, and your partner may have less stake in the venture's success because of its limited nature.

Joint Venture

The joint venture is the approach most favored by both the Vietnamese government and the international business community, accounting for some 71% of all foreign investment projects.

A joint venture contract signed between one or more foreign parties and one or more Vietnamese parties creates a new legal entity as a limited liability company.

Foreign capital may constitute as much as 99% of the company's total capital, and it must constitute at least 30%.

A joint venture contract and charter, as well as a feasibility study and a petition for preferential tax treatment, are to be submitted with the application.

Advantages The government favors this form of investment, so you may be more likely to be approved; you get the benefit of your local partner's knowledge of the Vietnamese market, and this partner may have access to land and a location you couldn't find on your own.

Disadvantages It can be hard to find a good partner; regulations give the local side major input into business and management decisions even if its share of capital is relatively small.

100% Foreign-Owned Enterprise

One measure of the extent to which international commerce has been liberalized in Vietnam is the fact that the country allows the establishment of companies with 100% foreign capital and those that are wholly owned and managed by the foreign investor. Such companies, which are created as new legal entities in Vietnam, constitute just under 18% of the foreign investment projects licensed to date.

Documents required with the application process include a feasibility study, a charter of the enterprise, documents relating to the investor's parent company, and a petition for preferential tax treatment.

Advantages There are fewer constraints in management and business decisions than with joint ventures, and you can't get tripped up by a bad partner.

Disadvantages You miss out on the know-how of a good partner, and government tolerates you but likes joint ventures better.

Build-Operate-Transfer (B.O.T.)

Amendments added to the investment code in late 1992 established a new procedure by which foreign investors contract with a Vietnamese government agency to build an infrastructure project, operate it for a period of time to recoup costs and make a profit, and then transfer it to the government without condition or compensation. Examples of B.O.T. projects in various stages of planning include hydroelectric power stations, bridges, water supply systems, and waste treatment facilities.

Advantages With regulations not fully detailed and infrastructure such a high priority, the approval process may be simplified and sped up; unlike other sectors, there's actually money in the pipeline (from international aid programs) to fund these projects.

Disadvantages According to Kathleen Charlton, BOT financing are still limited because many large infrastructure projects are not commercially feasible. For example, it would be difficult to finance a road or bridge BOT in Vietnam because passengers cannot afford to pay substantial tolls at this point. Another disadvantage is that the government might change its position after the infrastructure project is built. This happened with a highway project in Thailand.

Export Processing Zones

To further stimulate investment, encourage the manufacture of goods for export to earn foreign exchange, and promote economic development in particular regions, the government has established a number of export processing zones (EPZs), including the following:

1. Linh Trung EPZ in Ho Chi Minh City
2. Tan Thuan EPZ in Ho Chi Minh City
3. Da Nang EPZ

4. Hai Phong EPZ
5. Noi Bai EPZ in Hanoi
6. Vung Tau EPZ in Vung Tau
7. Can Tho EPZ in Can Tho

Other zones are expected to come on-line soon.

Investors are encouraged to establish manufacturing facilities in these zones, which produce goods for export. In return, they receive special tax preferences: a 10% profit tax rate after a four-year exemption beginning with the first profit-making year. For service companies, the tax rate is 15% with a two-year exemption.

In addition, there is an exemption from import/export duties and expedited access to water, power, and telecommunications.

Advantages There are lower taxes and a greater likelihood of being approved for a 100% foreign-owned company.

Disadvantages There are high rents and other costs and more stringent environmental regulations.

FORGING AHEAD: COMPLETING THE BUSINESS PLAN AND APPLICATION PROCESS

Let's suppose that you have

1. researched the market,
2. identified your opportunity,
3. perhaps established a foothold in the market by opening a representative office, and
4. selected the most advantageous method of investment.

You are now ready to move to the application process. Let's assume you have followed the pattern of most businesspeople and opted for a joint venture.

Partners

Your choice of a partner is critical (see the discussion of problems involving partners in chapter 7). In fact, many experts identify this decision as the single most important decision you will make in implementing your business plan.

The SCCI itself may steer you to a partner, as will the Vietnam Chamber, the ministry related to your industry sector, and local people's committees. In some cases the government agencies themselves or a company they directly control may become your partner. You can also unearth potential partners through the extensive market research and familiarization activities you have done in earlier steps. In any case, careful evaluation should be made prior to selecting a partner recommended by such organizations or committees.

Thomas Schwarz notes, "It is important for foreign companies to conduct proper due diligence prior to engaging a partner. This includes investigation into the domestic company's financial and commercial status." Schwarz also said that firms should consider talking to the commercial attaches of Eastern European embassies who already have a track record with local companies.

Land

Given that Vietnamese partners rarely have substantial amounts of money to invest with you, what do they bring to the table? In many cases, it is the land on which you will locate your business.

In Vietnam all land is owned by the people and administered by the state. This means that should you want to secure a property and build a hotel or factory on it, you are not permitted to actually buy the land, only to secure the right to rent it. The maximum allowable period of land use is currently 50 years, with terms of over 20 years subject to special approval by the prime minister.

Understandably, most land-use rights are held by Vietnamese entities of various kinds. Often a local partner is chosen essentially because of the site to which that partner has access.

For example, one would not expect the Ministry of Defense to be in the hotel business, yet the ministry is a joint venture partner in the Saigon Star Hotel. Why? Because when South Vietnam fell, the ministry came into possession of the military facilities of the United States and the Saigon governments. One of the sites caught the eye of investors, so they formed a partnership in which the Ministry of Defense contributed the building and site where the Saigon Star Hotel is now located!

One cautionary note. Make sure that if you are being promised a site that your potential partner really has an undisputed right to, transfer the use to your new joint venture company. When looking for land, foreign companies should check with the provincial people's committee about land use rights.

The Application Process

Applying for an investment license involves the preparation of a detailed feasibility study, budget, site proposal and construction plans, joint venture contract and charter, and other backup documents. (For specifications on what these should include, see the regulations reprinted in chapter 15 in the Resource Guide.)

As you prepare these documents, you should be, if you are not already, in constant communication and negotiation with the SCCI as well as the relevant ministry and people's committee. Your goal should be to work through the process in such a way that by the time you submit your finished application you have already heard and addressed any concerns raised as well as cultivated an interest in the project by the decision makers.

Normally, ten sets of the application documents are prepared: two are sent to the local people's committee and eight to the SCCI, which in turn will forward some to various ministries for approval. The SCCI will make a decision in three months. If approved, you will be issued a license—and your project will become duly recorded and chronicled as one more illustration of Vietnam's commitment to a market economy with a strong international presence!

5

HOW TO TRADE IN VIETNAM

"Opportunity does knock twice after all." That's how Landy Eng, a Chinese-American businessman based in Hong Kong, puts it.

> If you missed out on the opening of China because you were too young, too slow or had too little capital, Vietnam offers another chance. China is probably too big now for the individual entrepreneur and there is no particular interest in "Americanizing" the marketplace.
>
> In Vietnam, you have a strong residual identification with American brand names, a decentralized marketplace and a business climate where almost everybody, including the biggest U.S. multinationals are starting small. There are few if any at all "old Vietnam hands" like there are "old China hands" now. You will not be out of place.

Indeed, Mr. Eng, one of the pioneer traders in China in the late 1970s, describes himself as being "dragged into Vietnam" by irresistible opportunities and by his own network of business associates themselves anxious to crack the market. He is now busy locking up deals to sell a wide array of construction-related materials in Vietnam.

As the sector-by-sector review of opportunities in chapter 3 shows, many business opportunities in Vietnam do not involve building factories and bridges or opening up chains of retail outlets. Sure, that is what Vietnam wants to emphasize, as would any developing market economy with an excess of labor, a shortage of foreign exchange, and a crumbling infrastructure.

But what about the business that simply wants to find new customers and sell products to Vietnam without making a complex, long-term investment in the country? How can it be done?

To answer these questions, let's explore, one by one, the key policies, issues, and conditions that characterize Vietnam as an export market and international trader.

INSIGNIFICANT TRADE—UP TO NOW

In 1993, Vietnam's international commerce was essentially balanced but small compared to other trading nations and considering its size and potential.

The country exported approximately $3 billion, a 10% increase over 1992. Major exports are crude oil, rice, sea products, coffee and tea, rubber, textiles and garments, and ground nuts.

Imports increased 31.5% in 1993 over 1992, reaching $3.1 billion. Leading imports are electronic goods, fabrics, fertilizer, motor vehicles, and automotive parts.

Vietnam's scarcity of disposable income and foreign exchange, as well as years of central planning and international isolation, helps account for the country's small role in international trade. Yet, with rising incomes, massive rebuilding funded in large part by international aid, and substantial growth with controlled inflation triggered by market reforms, trade volume and opportunities will expand greatly in the near future.

Doi Moi in the International Trade Arena

Before *doi moi*, Vietnam's international trade was handled in a centralized fashion by state trading companies engaged primarily in barter trade with former communist bloc countries. This centrally planned system has undergone substantial change to a market-oriented system. As delineated by the Hong Kong Trade Development Council, in addition to the traditional general state trading companies are the following:

- Specialized state trading companies that emphasize certain products and sectors, such as food and electronics
- General provincial companies that emphasize a regional marketplace, such as Hanoi or the greater Saigon area
- Specialized provincial companies that further segment the market by both region and product
- Private companies that are licensed by the government to engage in certain trading activities

All told, there are now more than 500 companies licensed to trade in Vietnam, nearly triple the number in 1989. (A representative list of trading companies can be found in chapter 12 in the Resource Guide.)

The Ministry of Trade and Tourism is the key government agency responsible for the following:

- Implementing policies on importing and exporting, including issuing licenses, allocating commodities quotas, and publishing duty schedules and new regulations
- Assisting the foreign businessperson in identifying trade opportunities and customers and helping to double-check potential Vietnamese trading partners to ensure they are financially viable and licensed to import certain products. Note that caution should be used when obtaining such advice.
- Granting permission to foreign companies wishing to open representative offices in Vietnam

I have personally experienced a great deal of helpfulness with all my inquiries to this ministry. If nothing else, it is a good place to begin your market research and information-gathering process as the ministry is now accustomed to receiving hundreds of foreign trade delegations annually.

You can contact the ministry as follows:

In Hanoi: Ministry of Trade and Tourism
31 Trang Tien Street
Tel: 84- 42- 62529
Fax: 84- 42- 64696

In Ho Chi Minh City: Ministry of Trade and Tourism
35–37 Ben Chuong Duong, District 1
Tel: 84- 8-297316
Fax: 84- 8-291-011

A Rock and a Hard Place: High Tariffs and Smuggling

Whereas the regulatory scheme once relied more heavily on quotas, government policies are moving in the direction of liberalizing quotas and relying instead on tariffs to control imports.

Some items are banned for import into Vietnam. A recent government bulletin announced that the prime minister had decreed an import ban on the following:

- Weapons, ammunition, and explosives
- Military equipment
- Narcotics
- Poisonous chemicals
- "Reactionary and prurient cultural items"
- Fireworks
- Harmful toys
- Cigarettes
- All kinds of secondhand consumer goods, including garments, electrical appliances, cars with fewer than twelve seats, bicycles, motorcycles, and three-wheeled vehicles

The announcement concluded by noting that the "prime minister can grant exceptions"—although presumably he will not do so when it comes to "reactionary and prurient items"!

Import tariffs are generally high, particularly for items viewed as luxuries or as low-priority items that the government deems unessential to the country's development. Some examples are as follows:

- Fuels, raw materials, and construction materials—tariffs of zero to 5%
- Garments, electrical appliances, and electronics—tariffs of 40% to 60%
- Soft drinks, beer, and brandy—tariffs of 70%, 100%, and 150%, respectively

A complete, updated list of duties is available from the Ministry of Trade and Tourism.

There are some important exemptions from these tariffs. For many foreign business ventures, the exceptions to the rules are more relevant than the rules themselves. Duties are not levied on the following:

- Personal belongings, including vehicles brought in for use by resident expatriates
- Equipment for use in ongoing business operations of a joint venture
- Importation of materials for a construction project if those materials have been identified as part of the foreign party's capital contribution to that project
- Importation of materials to produce goods for export

High tariffs make exporting through official channels expensive for many products (particularly in a poor country), and when these high tariffs are coupled with large-scale smuggling through unofficial channels, it is easy to be priced right out of the market. The Vietnamese government has pledged to crack down on smuggling, but that is easier pledged than accomplished. Two key questions confronting anyone wanting to sell to Vietnam are, Is my product already for sale there through smuggling and third parties, and, If so, can I be priced competitively in a country with high tariffs and little disposable income?

Although Vietnamese highly value quality and status in their consumer purchases, cost by necessity remains the overriding factor driving most buying decisions.

VIETNAMESE MAY LIKE AMERICAN PRODUCTS MORE THAN AMERICANS DO!

If there is a redeeming quality to the extensive smuggling and reexporting of American and other foreign goods into Vietnam, it is that these activities have kept interest and demand high for the best-known brand names. Moreover, many families in the south have been receiving steady supplies of popular consumer products jammed into the oversized suitcases that their overseas relatives continually lug back home for family visits.

The result is a global rarity for American products—Vietnam, at least in the south, is almost Mexico-like in terms of the esteem, status, and desirability with which its consumers hold American brand names. If something comes from America, whether it be heavy construction machinery, computers, or candy, it is viewed as being of the best quality.

Journalist Robert Templor has described the phenomenon as a Vietnamese consumer love affair with the United States:

> The image of American goods may have diminished around the world but in Vietnam it remains lustrous, untarnished by contact during the nearly two decades of the U.S. trade embargo. . . . There is a high brand recognition for U.S. products, far higher than the economic sophistication of the country would suggest.

UNDERSTANDING THE VIETNAMESE CONSUMER

Because of ongoing links with Western cultures through the colonial years, the war years, and even during the embargo years, the sophistication of urban Vietnamese consumers, especially in the Saigon area, is very high considering the official average income level. The Vietnam Investment Information and Consulting firm reports the following:

- Products with high market penetration (85% to 100%) include laundry detergent, toothpaste,

seasoning, bath soap, health remedies, electric fans, instant noodles, and shampoo.
- Products with middle market penetration (65% to 80%) include televisions, candy, soft drinks, radios and cassette players, cigarettes, beer, and motor scooters.
- Products with low market penetration (20% to 30%) include liquor, milk powder, liquid dishwashing soap, videocassette recorders, and draft beer.

Vietnam is a land of extreme differences in wealth and life-style. Therefore, it is hard to generalize about the consumer. One expert guesses that just 15% of the population now possesses the necessary disposable income to even consider buying Western consumer goods. Yet, as discussed earlier, there is an emerging white-collar, cosmopolitan middle class in the major cities. Peeking into the typical consumer household in Ho Chi Minh City, you will most likely find the following:

- Five persons per household with an income of $480 per person per year (other estimates put urban middle-class income at $2,000 per year when factoring in underground activity and gifts from overseas)
- 72% of household income spent on food and drink
- A motorscooter but no car or telephone
- A television, video games, and probably a VCR
- Electric fans but no air conditioning
- Very little furniture, as most Vietnamese families live what we would term a communal life-style (e.g., no bedrooms for family members; meals enjoyed sitting on the floor or bunched around a small table with the food spread out family style in the middle)
- An eclectic assortment of products, household items, and luxury goods brought from U.S. relatives during family reunions

- A fondness for U.S. products as well as goods with an American identity, such as scenic calendars, books, and shirts with logos from the United States

One savvy way to determine what is most in demand in Vietnam is to ask overseas Vietnamese what they are most frequently asked to bring back home when they visit—money and gold aside! Some of the most requested items from visiting family members include the following:

- Baby supplies such as cribs, portable baths, and car seats
- Hand-held video games and the more sophisticated toys
- Designer jeans, sunglasses, and other prestige, status products
- Televisions, VCRs, portable generators (for the frequent power blackouts in Ho Chi Minh City), and small appliances such as rice cookers, hotplates, and electric thermoses
- Chocolate candy and other specialty food and personal care items such as colognes, perfume, makeup, and bath salts
- CD players and recorded music by Vietnamese-American pop stars and mainstream American singers

The Vietnamese consumers and those wishing to sell to them are learning more about each other every day. At the April 1994 Vietnamerica Expo, exhibitors gathered some basic market intelligence by gauging the reactions of attendees to their products. Even a company of such worldwide marketing sophistication as Pepsico learned, in the words of one of its snack food executives, that "Vietnamese like sweetened things, barbecue-flavored corn chips and many other American snacks, but not potato chips."

Don't Overlook Selling to the Sellers

Although Vietnamese consumers may not be flush with cash to buy upscale products, other foreigners establishing toeholds in Vietnam are bringing with them a panoply of needs. Many companies can find their niches by catering to a rapidly expanding tourist industry and expatriate community. Demand for Western-style consumer goods, housing and office facilities, foods and drinks, entertainment, appliances, vehicles, and household and office supplies are opening many opportunities.

The short-term payoff may be small, but, by selling to tourists and expatriates now, you would also be making a marketing investment in the future. Given the status and quality consciousness of the Vietnamese middle class, exposing your products in the market now may help generate demand among local residents as their disposable incomes grow.

Members of the California Table Grape Commission, for example, made an exploratory visit to Vietnam recently and concluded that although high-value products like table grapes may not have an immediate viability in the local market, there is potential as the tourist industry and related restaurant and hotel sectors expand.

Not All Trade Opportunities Have "Sex Appeal"

It is interesting and fun to talk about a "cola war" in Vietnam between Coke and Pepsi or chronicle the Vietnamese reaction as world-famous products like Honda motorbikes, Mercedes Benz cars, or MTV are introduced. Yet Vietnam is a land of much more basic needs, such as cement, paint, wire, pipes, cardboard packaging, machinery, and fertilizer.

Recognizing this, the Vietnamese government, while permitting importation of popular, high-value products, registers its lack of enthusiasm through its schedule of high tariffs. "It's just not the priority for us now," one Ministry of Trade official told me. Instead, the government has identified five areas of imports that are to be given priority both through low to near zero tariffs and through government-influenced buying decisions. These "strategic" areas are as follows:

- Refined petroleum products
- Fertilizers and agrochemicals
- Raw cotton, yarn, filaments, and raw materials related to textile production
- Spare parts for machinery
- Construction materials for infrastructure projects

International traders would be wise not to overlook Vietnam's basic needs. You are more likely to be able to get your foot in the door that way than you are by waiting for enough Vietnamese to become prosperous enough to buy expensive consumer products.

MARKETING AND DISTRIBUTION IN VIETNAM

The development of an efficient marketing and distribution network is in its infant stages in Vietnam.

Companies doing business in southern California remember well the disruptions caused by the severing of Interstate 5, the major north-south artery in the western United States, as a result of the January 1994 Northridge earthquake.

So imagine what it's like in Vietnam, where the lack of a suitable means of moving people and goods from north to south is an everyday fact of life! Neither train nor truck nor Russian-built airplane is available to any significant degree to transport products around the country.

That's why those wanting to sell products in Vietnam on a national basis must establish parallel distribution networks in different regions of the country. A better approach for all but the very largest firms is suggested by Tim Shepherd, the former executive director of the Vietnam Business Association of Hong Kong: "Develop a city strategy rather than a country strategy, at least until you get your feet wet and the infrastructure and distribution system improve."

The Hong Kong Trade Development Council estimates that "only one-third of the goods are transported by modern means such as truck, ships or rail within Vietnam. The rest are moved on bicycles, carts or small boats."

The point of sale for most products remains small stalls or kiosks at neighborhood marketplaces or family-run businesses on the ground floors or front rooms of their dwellings. This is why, despite the noise, dirt, and lack of privacy, urban residences directly fronting busy thoroughfares are highly prized real estate for Vietnamese families.

Recently, a number of modern showrooms displaying cars, appliances, hardware, and other products have made appearances in Ho Chi Minh City, though many Vietnamese seem uncomfortable entering them. The ones I have visited always seemed to be empty.

Trade shows, seminars, and exhibitions are becoming more familiar means of communicating product information to potential Vietnamese buyers. The Vietnam Chamber of Commerce and Industry organizes a calendar of trade shows and exhibitions in both Hanoi and Ho Chi Minh City covering a broad range of products and sectors. For a current calendar of shows, contact the chambers as follows:

In Hanoi: 33 Ba Trieu Street
              Tel: 84- 42-59325
              Fax: 84- 42-56446
              Attn: Mr. Duong Ky Anh

In Ho Chi Minh City: 171 Vo Thi Sau Street, District 3
Tel: 84-8-230-339
Fax: 84-8-294-472
Attn: Ms. Bui Thi Thuc Anh

Organizations outside Vietnam, such as the San Diego–based Vietnam Investment Information and Consulting firm and Hong Kong–based Infocus, also organize programs in Vietnam to bring foreign suppliers together with Vietnamese buyers.

Direct consumer marketing relies primarily on billboards, word of mouth, residual brand-name recognition, and some television and radio advertising. Like most other economic activities in Vietnam, both marketing and distribution are labor intensive and inefficient, with few economies of scale being realized. Large numbers of people are required to sell and distribute the product, almost shop by shop and consumer by consumer. Products requiring extensive postsale servicing require even greater painstaking commitment and involvement "on the ground."

This is why it is critical for those wishing to export to Vietnam to choose their partners well, be they direct customers, trading companies, distribution companies, or your own locally hired sales force. The Ministry of Trade, the Vietnam Chamber of Commerce and Industry, and your own contacts among the local business community all can help you determine who might want to buy your product and how you're going to get it to them.

GETTING PAID

You are probably also interested in the minor question of how you are going to get paid! The Hong Kong Trade Development Council identified the problem of payment as one of the key obstacles remaining in exporting to Vietnam. The group summarizes the issue this way:

Companies seeking to open letters of credit (L/C) to finance imports into Vietnam are subject to strict rules regarding deposit of margins in foreign currencies to cover their payments. Applicants for L/C "at sight" must now deposit 100% in foreign currency with the issuing bank before the L/C can be issued. "Usance" L/C however can be issued on a smaller margin, usually between 30–50%.

Vietnamese L/Cs may not always be accepted. This is despite the fact that the situation has been improving and international banks have been providing facilities for clients exporting to Vietnam. International banks with representative offices in Vietnam are often involved in verifying the nature of the transaction and the financial status of the Vietnamese importer. They also provide facilities for the confirmation of L/Cs.

It is advisable to state clearly in the contract (with as much detail as possible) the terms of payment, specifications, packing methods, until price and delivery date.

Vinacontrol (the Vietnam Superintendence and Inspection Company) is the entity that has been set up for the independent inspection and certification of imports and exports. Vinacontrol can be contacted as follows:

In Hanoi: 54 Tran Nhan Tong Street
            Tel: 84- 42-53840
            Cable: VINACONTROL HANOI

In Ho Chi Minh City: 80 Ba Huyen Thanh Quan Street
                       Tel: 84- 8-244-322
                       Telex: 812671 VINACO VT

How to Register Trademarks

In recognition of the importance of protecting intellectual property worldwide, even in the absence of a business presence, the U.S. government allowed American firms to register their trademarks despite the existence of the embargo. Now that the embargo has been lifted, the principle is the same: owners of intellectual property should take steps to protect that property in the free-wheeling business climate of Vietnam even if they don't plan to transact business there any time soon.

Although the concept of private ownership of intellectual property rights is relatively new in Vietnam, Vietnamese law recognizes such rights with the following periods of protection:

- 10 years for trademarks (renewable for an additional 10 years)
- 8 years for utility solutions
- 5 years for industrial designs
- 15 years for inventions

The application procedure is similar for all categories. We will focus on trademarks, as this is the priority for traders, particularly in the early stages of Vietnam's economic development.

Trademarks registered with the former government of South Vietnam were recognized following the country's reunification in 1975, but those not renewed by now have elapsed.

The Vietnamese government has established the National Office of Inventions (NOI) within the State Committee for Science and Technology in Hanoi to administer the registration and recording of trademarks. Application for the registration of trademarks may be made directly to NOI if the applicant has an establishment in Vietnam. If not, application must be made through the Vietnam Chamber of Commerce and Industry or another authorized Vietnamese industrial property agent, such as Invenco. Thomas Schwarz states that the government has authorized 10 organizations—trade groups, consultants and law firms—to represent companies seeking trademark protection.

Vietnam follows a "first to file" rather than a "first to use" approach to trademarks, which has caused some problems for some internationally known products. There have been cases of local Vietnamese snapping up trademark registrations and then waiting for the surprised original owner of the trademark to come knocking at their door!

The registration process usually entails a trademark search so that any possible objections or conflicts can be discovered and hopefully resolved in advance.

Applicants are also advised to develop Vietnamese-language equivalents of their trademarks and register those as well. This prevents a local company from adopting the Vietnamese equivalent of your trademark and cashing in on your product's reputation.

Once the completed application is made, the NOI is supposed to give you an answer within six months and must state a reason if the application is denied.

If the application is approved, a registration certificate is issued, and your trademark is entered in the National Register of Marks.

The trademark is valid for 10 years, although it may be canceled if not used in Vietnam for a period of five years. The registration can be renewed through reapplication six months prior to the date of expiration.

Fees, including payment to the agent, are $180 per class for registration, $170 per class for renewal, and $105 for claiming convention priority. Agency fees are 50% higher for a collective trademark.

Vietnamese law also empowers a number of government agencies, in addition to the NOI, to help enforce trademark protection by punishing—through administrative actions, fines, and criminal prosecution—those who engage in counterfeiting. Although many violators of intellectual property rights get away with it, foreign companies with complaints have successfully engaged the help of Vietnamese authorities to stop violations. The government appears to be taking the issue seriously.

Vietnam is a member of the Paris Convention for the Protection of Industrial Property and the Madrid Agreement Concerning the International Registration of Marks; also, it follows the International Classification of Goods and Services.

EVENTUALLY, TRADE MUST BECOME A TWO-WAY STREET

No sooner had the U.S. trade embargo been lifted than the "talking points" of Vietnamese officials I spoke with shifted to their new priority in the economic arena, namely, achieving most-favored nation (MFN) trading status. "Trade should not be a one-way street," I was told. Yet, without MFN status, Vietnamese imports in the United States are made uncompetitive because of higher tariffs.

It is unlikely that a move to grant MFN trading status to Vietnam will be advanced before the next U.S. presidential election in 1996. Emotion and politics are still too wrapped up in any decision concerning Vietnam, particularly one that would have the appearance of bestowing a "favor" on our former enemy.

This is unfortunate because in fact the importation and marketing of certain Vietnamese products would generate numerous business opportunities for Americans, particularly Vietnamese-Americans. There is a lucrative market niche for attractively packaged and marketed products from Vietnam that would not only cater to nostalgic Vietnamese but would also satisfy a more general demand for Asian products. Vietnamese handicrafts and other cultural items—as well as spices, seafood products, rice, and coffee marketed as specialty food products—could do well in the urban centers of North America.

Then there's the issue of leverage in future trade talks with the Vietnamese. The fact that the United States maintains significant barriers, comparatively speaking, to Vietnamese products makes it difficult for American businesspeople and trade negotiators to lobby the Vietnamese with credibility as to the improvements they could make in their own trade and investment policies.

Hopefully, trade between the United States and Vietnam will soon become a "two-way street" and benefit citizens on both shores of the Pacific.

Steps and Strategies for Trade with Vietnam

Having discussed the policies, trends, considerations, and challenges that characterize the Vietnamese trading system, what approaches to entering the market are best for you? What steps should you take?

Some Important Questions

To determine whether and how you should proceed, you must ask yourself some questions that ultimately only you can answer:

- Have you ever exported before?
- Do you or your team have experience in Asian markets?
- Are you familiar with setting up a distribution network in a foreign country?
- If you have been using an export management company for other markets, does your exporter have capabilities in Vietnam? Or must you look elsewhere for the expertise?
- How far are you prepared to go? Are you interested simply in making a sale? Or do you and your firm

want to get on the ground yourselves, establishing your own distribution network, sales force, warehousing, and marketing? At what stage does the cost of the effort exceed the potential payoff?
- And finally, what do you do? And where do you go when the checklist says "Stop!"

Many of the steps and options outlined in the previous chapter are relevant to the exporter as well. Make an exploratory trip to Vietnam or assign your sales representative to go there and spend the necessary time researching the market. Continually cross-check your findings with your responses to the questions above.

A Vietnam Trade Checklist

As the Chinese market opened up in the late 1970s, Landy Eng developed a China trade checklist, which he has now adapted to Vietnam. As you conduct your market research and develop initial strategies, keep in mind these key points:

1. Match Vietnam's needs to your existing products.
2. Develop new product concepts for the Vietnamese market.
3. Offer management, training, and technical assistance with products.
4. Present well-focused and detailed seminars.
5. Understand your host trade organization and develop close rapport.
6. Know your competition and its products.
7. Recommend financing alternatives in your discussions.
8. Utilize Vietnamese-speaking staff members whenever possible.

9. Understand Vietnamese values, attitudes, and sensitivities.
10. Obtain professional advice.

Stages of Involvement: How Dirty Do You Want to Get Your Hands?

Your assessment of both the short- and the long-term potential of your products in Vietnam, as well as the cost and effort to realize that potential, will determine how fast and how far you want to move.

Stage 1 At the low end of involvement, you can basically "sit at home." Work through export management companies and access trade lead systems made available by the U.S. Department of Commerce as well as state organizations to see whether there are buyers for your products who will then take the responsibility for getting them to the Vietnamese market.

Stage 2 You can seek or entertain offers from a growing number of enterprising entrepreneurs from the United States, Hong Kong, and Singapore who will propose that they represent and distribute your products in Vietnam. This may be an acceptable short-term alternative for those who can't spare the resources to do it themselves or who want to test the waters first. Obviously, the background and capabilities of the group you work with, not to mention the terms, need to be carefully examined.

But you should also remember that Vietnam is such a new market that you may not find a specialist in your field right away. Be willing to work with the entrepreneurs who can prove to you that they have the networks, sophistication, and experience in other Asian markets and can move quickly! These are the people who made money for themselves and their clients in China while many of the larger, more established trading, distribution, and service companies spent endless amounts of time and your money doing feasibility studies.

Stage 3 You can seek sales directly in Vietnam from those who want to buy your product, locating major customers and signing contracts. Some firms put this process in motion by opening a representative office that has the responsibility of networking with all the appropriate local powers and potential customers. You can test this concept by making contact with the appropriate ministries and trading companies (public and private) that you determine might need your product or want to import and distribute it.

In addition to utilizing the organizations itemized in the Resource Guide, you can pinpoint local entities operating in your field by consulting the Ministry of Trade, the Vietnam Chamber of Commerce and Industry, the Hanoi and Ho Chi Minh City Yellow Pages, and other business directories. (To find out how to tap these resources, see chapters 12–14 in the Resource Guide.)

Finding the right Vietnamese trading partner is one of the most important steps in cracking this market. The proliferation of companies licensed to trade is a necessary step, but it also means that many newer companies lack experience and are probably undercapitalized. Mr. Dinh Van Hoi, a senior official with the Ministry of Trade in Hanoi, asked me to advise readers to make sure they investigate their business partners carefully. Can your Vietnamese partners do what they say they can? Are they really licensed to engage directly in importing and exporting the line of products you want to sell? The Ministry of Trade, the Vietnam Chamber, and your partner's bank are all places to cross-check their ability to follow through on commitments.

In addition, virtually every ministry in the Vietnamese government has some companies under its control. Under the aegis of the Ministry of Construction, for example, is the Materials Trading and Building Materials

Import-Export Company. Director Le Nghia Vu told me that his company not only buys a whole range of products from many countries for use in government projects but also imports them for distribution to a broad range of customers throughout Vietnam.

Stage 4 After testing the waters to various degrees in stages 1 through 3, you may determine that the potential is so good that just making a sale isn't good enough. You want to set up a distribution and marketing system with warehouses, showrooms, a sales force, and a consumer marketing plan. The best approach is to explore a joint venture arrangement with the kind of Vietnamese entities you worked with in stage 3.

Stage 5 Finally, companies who know they want to have a long-term, national marketing strategy in Vietnam may actually want to make the product in Vietnam for sale to the domestic market. Pepsico is a good example of a company that leapfrogged the stages of involvement and moved quickly to bottle directly in the country, working with an existing Vietnamese beverage company.

Whether this is the right strategy depends on the product and Vietnam's capabilities in addition to your own. Boeing, for example, has a stake and potential in this market that likely is even greater than that of Pepsi. Yet, it is hard to imagine Boeing aircraft or components being manufactured in Vietnam for a long time.

Vietnam is a frontier marketplace, offering all the excitement and challenges that living on the frontier creates. Success takes hard work, improvisation, risk, and patience. A certain breed of businessperson thrives in this atmosphere. Others prefer to stay closer to home or to operate in markets where their comfort level is greater. By moving in a staged fashion at a pace that is right for you, you can determine whether Vietnam is the right market for you and hopefully share in the excitement and capture some of the profits!

6

Understanding the Vietnamese Business Culture

The Vietnamese have a saying that sets the stage for this chapter: *Nhap gia tuy tuc* (pronounced "nyap ya twee took": "When you come into a new country, you have to follow the culture.").

Generalizing about the values, customs, and attitudes of any group is risky because it is easy to cross the line into simplistic or unfair stereotypes. Such generalities are also infused with the culture of the person making them. For example, if we come from a society that likes to get right down to business and we're dealing with one that does not, in our view that society is "slow." Yet a person from another culture with an even more time-consuming process would view the same one as "fast."

With that caveat, in the broadest terms, the international business community generally describes the Vietnamese as follows:

- Proud and nationalistic, believing fiercely that the "Vietnamese way" of doing things is the best way but often wary and even critical of one another.
- Smart, hardworking, eager to learn, and intensely determined to perform well—as long as they believe that they are being treated with respect and without condescension
- Compared to the Chinese and Japanese, more informal but more direct, easygoing, and overtly emotional while being less obsessed with hierarchy and order; at the same time, every bit as concerned with gaining and "saving face" as the Japanese, leading at times to exaggerated claims of importance, promises that cannot be kept, and difficulty saying no
- Unschooled in Western business practices and demeanor but tough, wily negotiators, sometimes changing terms and offers midstream; slow moving in terms of coming to closure on agreements and deals
- Less "sexist" and "racist" than other Asian societies in the way we understand those terms but far from adopting the avowed standards of the United States

Moving from the general to the specific, let's examine the Vietnamese business culture and how you should conduct yourself in it from a number of facets.

Names

In Vietnam, the last name comes first, followed by the middle name and first name. The problem is that there are very few surnames. It is estimated that over 50% of the entire population is named "Nguyen," roughly pronounced "n'win." Therefore, Vietnamese rely primarily

Understanding the Vietnamese Business Culture

on their first names to address one another but not without affixing Mr., Mrs., Miss, or Madame in front.

For example, if I were Vietnamese, I would introduce myself and sign my name as Robinson William James. I would then expect to be addressed as Mr. James.

Many Americans are familiar with the name of former South Vietnamese President Nguyen Van Thieu, who was often referred to as President Thieu. Equate that to the United States, and it would be the same as saying President Bill or former President George.

Military personnel have their first names, not their last, affixed to the fronts of their uniforms. Even the residential sections of Vietnamese phone books list subscribers in alphabetical order—by first name! That's because a directory made up almost entirely of Nguyens, Trans, Phams, and Les would be virtually useless.

So if a Vietnamese introduces himself to you as, say, Nguyen Huu Duc, he is telling you his last name, middle name, and first name, in that order. You should then refer to him as Mr. Duc, or, if he carries a particular title, it would be appropriate to refer to him as Mr. Director or Mr. Minister.

There are exceptions to the last-name-first custom. Most overseas Vietnamese have adopted the custom of their new homeland, putting the first name first. Yet, when they return home and meet local Vietnamese, they revert to the Vietnamese way.

The principle is the same for women, although you won't know at first whether to refer to her as Miss or Mrs. (I have never heard Ms. used in Vietnam!) Use Miss followed by the first name until you have determined whether she is married. Then use Mrs. or, as is still frequently done, Madame.

Even though necessity and tradition require the use of first names, you should continue to use the polite form of address (Mr., Miss, or Mrs.) long after you would have switched to first names only in a Western business relationship.

As for making your own introduction, maintain your Western ways and introduce yourself by your first name first and then your last name. Your Vietnamese counterparts will then address you politely, either by your first name (as in Mr. Bob or Miss Susan) or by your last name.

DRESSING FOR BUSINESS IN VIETNAM

Vietnamese chuckle at the sight of foreign businesspeople walking down the sweltering, dusty streets of Saigon in suits and ties. They may look nice, but they feel miserable!

Most Vietnamese dress informally. The typical office "uniform" for men consists of dress slacks with a short-sleeve white shirt. Some wear ties, particularly those of higher rank. Women almost always wear skirts or the more traditional *ao dai* (pronounced "ow yai")—a colorful smocklike pullover that is worn over white slacks.

Recently, as the economy has improved and Vietnam grows more cosmopolitan (and as air conditioning improves!), business attire has become more formal. When meeting with senior government and business executives, you are now more likely to find your counterpart in a Western-style suit, but this is still an exception to the rule.

How should *you* dress? My rule of thumb is that if you are unsure, err on the side of overdressing rather than underdressing:

- For ceremonial functions and meetings with senior officials, men should wear lightweight suits and women dresses or skirts.
- For meetings at lower levels with functionaries, no jacket is required, but I still find a tie appropriate.

Understanding the Vietnamese Business Culture

It is acceptable for women on these occasions to dress in tasteful slacks outfits, but most do not.

- For follow-up meetings where you have determined that greater informality is the rule, you can be informal as well and leave the necktie at your hotel, although Eugene Matthews requires that his male employees wear a tie at all times. Should you be invited for after-hours drinks or dinner, the atmosphere is almost always informal. You don't need to wear a suit—slacks and a shirt will do.

CONDUCT AND APPROACH IN MEETINGS

Private offices are a rarity in Vietnam. When you arrive for a meeting, you will usually be escorted to a small conference room that, thankfully, is often the only room in the office that is air conditioned. You and your party sit on one side of the table and your hosts on the other. Tea or coffee will be brought automatically.

Meetings open with handshakes and the exchange of business cards. Offer your card with both hands, and the lettering on the card should face right side up for the person you are greeting. He or she will do the same. Kathleen Charlton points out that it is important to shake hands and exchange cards with the most senior person at the meeting first. (This rule also applies to the final handshake.) Take a moment to study the card respectfully, look at the person, and perhaps offer an additional greeting. To keep names and faces straight, it is acceptable for you to spread the cards in front of yourself when seated, but you should not make notes on the cards, as this is a sign of disrespect.

On the basis of many meetings he has been in, Ross Dunkley of the *Vietnam Investment Review* finds the

Vietnamese by nature more informal than other Asian peoples but often nervous at the outset of the initial meeting. He summarizes the guidelines he follows this way, and I concur:

> In meetings, never discuss business first. Have a general discussion first. In fact, I would say don't even try to do business in the first meeting. In some cultures, business is the first thing you get to. In Vietnam it's usually the last thing you get to. You aren't going to get the Vietnamese to move any faster than they want to anyway. Always keep your voice down and speak in humble, respectful tones.

It is good to begin a meeting with a short statement thanking your hosts for their time and stating your purpose in very general, diplomatic terms. Translating is required at most meetings, as even Vietnamese who speak some English are shy and unsure about it. As they grow more comfortable with you, their use of English tends to increase and improve. I have been in many meetings that began with translation, but by the end no translation seemed necessary. You should plan to bring a Vietnamese-speaking person to your meeting unless you can ascertain in advance that a bilingual individual is available at the organization you are visiting.

Gift giving at an initial meeting is not necessary and generally is not done unless you have some small memento particular to your company or organization. If you spend a good deal of time with one individual (e.g., a representative of a people's committee or chamber who has taken you around to various meetings), then a small gift—such as a bottle of whiskey, some perfume, or a book of scenic photographs from your home state or country—is an appreciated gesture.

Most meetings follow this general pattern. Overall I have found Vietnamese in this setting friendly and informal but not immediately open or engaging in personal comments. They are curious about life in your home country and sometimes possess a surprising degree of knowledge about it. At a recent meeting at a ministry in Hanoi, I was surprised to be asked some lighthearted questions about "Whitewater"!

Unless you say something extremely insulting and inappropriate in a meeting, it is hard to make a serious mistake simply by violating some mysterious, unwritten rules of Vietnamese protocol.

SMOKING AND DRINKING

Most Vietnamese men smoke with a vengeance. Women never do, at least not in public. "Political correctness" regarding smoking has not yet reached Vietnam, and you can expect to encounter smoking at any time and in any place, including in the middle of meals. Forget about finding a no-smoking section at the restaurant. You will be lucky if you are sitting at a no-smoking table!

Your Vietnamese hosts may possibly light up during meetings. Often a fresh pack of cigarettes and an ashtray sits at the center of the table in the conference room. Your host may ceremoniously open the pack and offer you a cigarette before lighting up himself.

During my most recent visit, I observed a few no-smoking signs in meeting rooms. Smoking has also been banned on all domestic Vietnam Airlines flights. Slowly, an antismoking consciousness is starting to take shape.

Beer (often served over ice), whiskey, and imported cognac are the favored drinks when socializing. Drinking after work and over dinner can be an important method of bonding with business acquaintances, but it is not a "command performance" as it often feels like when you are carousing the bars with the Japanese in Tokyo or downing toast after toast with the Chinese at a banquet in Beijing. If you don't wish to imbibe, no one else at the table will give it much of a thought or try to push you.

A Woman's Perspective

There are women in senior governmental and business positions in Vietnam, although men easily outnumber women in these positions. Through decades of colonialism, civil war, deprivation, and social upheaval, Vietnamese women have often been left to fend for themselves. Out of necessity, they have long undertaken tasks, including very physical ones, that in other societies are seen as "man's work."

Vietnamese women are treated with respect and are less likely to be seen simply as sex objects compared to both Asian and Western societies. Trying to be "one of the boys" by speaking in coarse, earthy terms about Vietnamese women is considered to be in very poor taste. Comparatively speaking, Vietnamese are more conservative, reserved, and shy about sex and sexual topics.

As for foreign women doing business or operating in Vietnam, Shawna Stonehouse, managing director of Infocus, has had extensive dealings in the country and knows other women with experience there as well. She has perceived no problems being taken seriously in Vietnam. She has observed that in informal settings, such as business dinners or receptions, Vietnamese men are flirtatious in a gentle, harmless sort of way, but the society as a whole "is less sexist than most."

Relationships

Hong Kong businessman Paul Ho has done business in Vietnam for 20 years. He and his partner in Vietnam, Henry Ha, both underscore the role that close contacts and friendships have played in their own successful ventures and in others they have observed: "The Vietnamese are highly loyal to old friends," Mr. Ho told me. "Build relationships first and you will be more successful and avoid problems down the line."

Ross Dunkley of the *Vietnam Investment Review* echoes this: "The secret of success is to build up personal relations. Get them to understand you are a friend and try to do something together that is genuinely good for everybody."

Following Through

Establishing a good contact base in Vietnam is easy to say but not so simple to accomplish when you live half a world away. Indeed, a number of businesspeople told me that the most common mistake they see being made by foreigners is the failure to follow through: "They fly in for a week, have a bunch of meetings, exude enthusiasm and state grandiose intentions—and then poof they're gone," is how one American now based in Hanoi described other Americans testing the waters. "Then, some even come back six months later and wonder why nothing has happened yet. The Vietnamese are starting to get tired of all this."

Cultivate your contacts and establish your own trustworthiness by being gracious and respectful and never promising more in the excitement of the moment than you really intend. If you promise to send some information or follow up on a question posed to you, be sure to make good on that promise! Kathleen Charlton, Managing Director of Ashta International, points out how important it is to follow up with thank you letters and any materials you may have promised: "Vietnamese at all levels of government and business are hungry for outside information."

Mr. Dunkley and others go even further, saying that "the only sure way to understand the business culture and establish the necessary relations is to be here. Get yourself on the ground in Vietnam. Spend some time here. Don't rely on anyone else to do it for you."

EQUAL TREATMENT VERSUS CONDESCENSION

"Vietnamese can sense condescension a mile off, and it's the worst mistake you can make with them," according to an American businessman operating in Vietnam. All people like to be treated with respect, but Vietnamese, given their history of being under the domination of foreigners, are more sensitive to the lack of it than most.

Henry Ha told me that of all the varied advice he could give to those just starting out in Vietnam, the most important would be the need for "equal treatment." He explains, "Treat the Vietnamese well and with respect and they will do almost anything for you. You will have their complete loyalty."

TALKING POLITICS AND PERSONAL VIEWS

Although Vietnamese are generally friendly and relaxed, these qualities often mask a wary nature underneath that does not invite personal inquiries. A standard nostrum about doing business in Asia, for example, is to ask about their families. Yet I have not found Vietnamese in the early stages of a business relationship to be particularly forthcoming about their families or curious about yours.

As for the war, Vietnamese tell westerners that they have put it behind them and want to look to the future, but painful scars remain. The war is not a taboo subject. There is nothing wrong with referring to it in a matter-of-fact way or to pose technical or historical questions about it. But be cautious in discussing opinions of the war or asking personal questions about your hosts' own wartime experiences. In addition, you should not put them on the spot by asking their opinions about government policies. Let the Vietnamese be the ones to raise any of these subjects.

Don't forget that the war meant different things to different people. You may be talking to someone who secretly despises the current government or who was actually stripped of property and imprisoned after the war. Criticizing your own government's wartime policies or making pronouncements such as "In the long run the outcome was better for everyone" may not score the points you think you are earning. You may be making a tactical error.

Many Vietnamese believe that Americans are obsessed with the war. They have concluded that this obsession has blocked good relations with the United States and blinded Americans to understanding Vietnam as a country and a people. There is no need to confirm their stereotype with continual references to that tragic chapter.

Is It Saigon or Ho Chi Minh City?

Although the former South Vietnamese capital has been officially renamed Ho Chi Minh City, the word *Saigon* has hardly been purged from the nation's vocabulary. The government-owned tourist agency is called Saigontourist. The river running through the city is still called the Saigon River. There are hotels and companies with the word *Saigon* in their names. The internationally accepted three-letter code for the city's airport is not HCM but SGN, just as it was before 1975.

What should you call Vietnam's most populous city and most important commercial center? When meeting with government ministries and affiliated organizations, you should refer to it as Ho Chi Minh City. Do the same in all written communication. When referring to the central part of town as a physical locale as opposed to an administrative unit, it is acceptable to call it Saigon. When talking with overseas Vietnamese, they would prefer you use the old name. Many make it a point to refuse to use the new name, for understandable reasons.

You can also take a cue from your Vietnamese counterpart. If he or she starts referring to the city as Saigon, you should feel free to do the same. It happens a lot. When in doubt, play it safe and say Ho Chi Minh City.

The North-South Split

Vietnamese will tell you at great length and in great detail of the vast cultural differences between North and South Vietnam, differences ingrained over the course of centuries. For international businesspeople, some differences in dealing in Hanoi as opposed to Ho Chi Minh City are apparent. Chiefly, the southern metropolis has a more international flavor and has had far greater exposure over the years to outside influences. Being the business center, it is also more prone to and accepting of rapid change, as it is being shaped by a greater influx of new people and ideas. Most foreigners, while appreciating the superior physical beauty of Hanoi, feel far more at home in Saigon. Eugene Matthews, however, prefers Hanoi to Saigon, stating that "Ho Chi Minh City could exist in most other Southeast Asian countries, while Hanoi is uniquely Vietnamese."

Until recently, Hanoi and the north had been in a state of communist isolation since 1954. This partially explains why many of the people you deal with are more reserved and stiff yet more dignified than their southern counterparts. But is also explains the differences in demeanor and personality between people of the north and south that have been long observed by Vietnam watchers.

Delineating these differences, the *Far Eastern Economic Review*'s Vietnam correspondent Murray Hiebert writes, "Many observers see significant personality differences, viewing southerners as more open-minded and adventurous. 'Northerners are upright, traditional and conservative,' argues an overseas Vietnamese businessman working in Ho Chi Minh City. 'Southerners are easygoing and loud-mouthed. Northerners are like the British, while southerners are like Australians.'"

FACE

The Asian concept of gaining and saving face—establishing one's worth and esteem in the eyes of others and avoiding disgrace and embarrassment—is extremely important to Vietnamese. Your social antenna should be finely tuned to sensing situations in which your counterpart may lose face and helping to find a way out of embarrassment for them.

There is another important reason to be alert to situations in which words and actions are designed to save face, namely, so that you can determine the true thoughts and intentions behind what you are being told.

Face creates some problems for up-front "tell-it-like-it-is" westerners. A Vietnamese may agree with you because he doesn't want to disagree, not because he really intends to do what he just agreed to! He may say he understands when he really doesn't. And he may make commitments before he is sure he can live up to them. Failing to perceive or understand these situations in business interactions with Vietnamese has led some westerners to complain about duplicity and dishonesty.

PATIENCE-PERSISTENCE-PERSEVERANCE

Dealing with intricate concepts such as "face" is just one reason why Ernst & Young's John Harvey thinks of the "three Ps" when advising clients on how to operate successfully in Vietnam's business culture: patience, persistence, and perseverance. Many others I spoke to emphasized that patience is the most important quality to maintain when operating in Vietnam.

Few Vietnamese are trained in Western-style business practices and telephone and office etiquette. Some manifestations of this inexperience seem minor, but it's those little things we take for granted that, when not performed the way we are used to, add up to frustration.

For example, it is customary in most business circles to answer faxes and phone calls, if nothing else, for the sake of courtesy. Vietnamese may not answer your fax simply because it is too expensive ($10 to $15 to send a page to the United States), because they don't understand who you are and what you want, or because they don't want to see you but don't want to tell you "no."

On a recent visit to Ho Chi Minh City, simply trying to call someone at another hotel to leave a message was a half-hour process—something that might take a minute back home. First, it took a number of tries to get through the busy signal. When the call went through, I had to spell out the name of the party several times before the hotel operator (at one of the best hotels, by the way!) could understand it. When there was no answer in the guest's room, I was disconnected before getting an opportunity to leave a message. I called back, explained that I wanted to leave a message, and then had to spell out the entire message twice! Patience, persistence, perseverance!

The goal of that admittedly minor ordeal was to leave a phone message. Magnify those frustrations 100-fold when you are attempting to move all the way from A to Z on a major business transaction involving several private parties and government bureaucracies! Patience, persistence, perseverance!

Change, Flexibility, and Pragmatism

When it comes to the "three Ps," history has shown that nobody does it better than the Vietnamese. They have persisted and persevered by being both infinitely patient as well as pragmatic and flexible. These attributes mitigate some of the frustration inherent in doing business in Vietnam because you know that most of the frustrations will be addressed. The Vietnamese have an enormous appetite to learn, to make things work better, and to work extremely hard. They may believe that there is a "Vietnamese way" of doing things, but the Vietnamese way is one of constant change.

Despite deep roots in the traditions of Confucius, Vietnam is not a static society locked into ancient ways. It is a dynamic society. Millions of people come and go, moving from north to south or around the world. Those once high and mighty have at different points in Vietnamese history found themselves lowly and insignificant. Those from insignificant families have risen to great prominence. Doctors and engineers may now be street merchants. Jungle-dwelling soldiers may now be running vast government bureaucracies. Refugees who just 15 to 20 years ago escaped with the clothes on their backs by walking across Cambodia or setting sail for the open seas are returning to visit, many sporting new families and new occupations. Like many Americans, many Vietnamese have reinvented themselves several times over the course of their lifetimes.

However unsettling and costly this has been to Vietnamese society, it has given the culture a dynamism that can serve it well adapting to and thriving in the competitive global economy. Having the will and the courage to change is not just rhetoric in Vietnam but has been reality and the key to survival. Equally important to the culture as the ability to be flexible is the emphasis placed on the family. It is through the family that sound values and a strong work ethic have been passed down.

7

PROBLEMS AND PITFALLS

A foreign banker in Vietnam was quoted by the *Far East Economic Review* as observing that on arriving in the country "hard-headed businessmen tend to forget their head. While looking at nirvana, you need to be sure not to miss the 10-foot pothole in front of you."

As an emerging market feeling its way along the path of market reform, Vietnam is doing many things right. The architect of modern Singapore, former Prime Minister Lee Kuan Yew, has boldly predicted that Vietnam "will be able to grow as fast as China with fewer mistakes."

Perhaps so, yet no one disputes that mistakes have been made and that some serious shortcomings in the business climate remain. Companies assessing the Vietnamese market need to know up front what the major hurdles are and how to factor them into their costs.

Some of the problems have been alluded to in other chapters. The purpose of this one is to itemize the major concerns.

The Legal System

As the *Wall Street Journal* summarizes it, "Many foreign investors have learned the hard way that the legal system is incomplete and inadequate. Worse, the interpretation of particular laws can vary from one week to the next." The newspaper recounts a case in which a Singaporean company prevailed in court in a commercial dispute, only to discover that winning didn't really matter because there was no mechanism by which the judgment could be enforced.

A recent survey of Korean investors in Vietnam found that the lack of clear, consistent laws and functioning mechanisms for enforcing those laws was their number one concern, bar none.

Practically speaking, this means that if you are engaged in a dispute with a partner, supplier, customer, or government agency, your avenues of legal recourse are extremely limited and ill-defined.

Price Waterhouse reports that in place of a proper court system for handling civil disputes, economic arbitration committees are set up by the various people's committees. Considering that your dispute may be with a company *owned* by a given people's committee, you may wonder about the objectivity of the arbitration panels!

All the analysts I spoke with echoed the same thought. "If you are making a foreign investment in Vietnam and/or entering into a commercial transaction of any kind, you must leave no stone unturned in spelling out the rights and obligations of the parties in clear and inclusive detail. Nothing must be left to chance."

Price Waterhouse adds, "Foreign investors would be well advised to negotiate the procedures for conflict resolution with their business partners and include them explicitly in the relevant contract."

Vietnamese policymakers are aware of this issue and have pledged to construct adequate legal mechanisms to protect businesses as quickly as possible. At the end of

1993, for example, a bankruptcy law was enacted that aimed to protect the legal interests of creditors. Despite having some shortcomings, this law has been greeted as an important, welcome step.

BUREAUCRACY, RED TAPE, AND ROVING REGULATIONS

Vietnam is surely not the only country where businesspeople are hampered by excessive bureaucracy, red tape, and continually changing rules and procedures. Yet confronting these problems in Vietnam has taken the glow off the marketplace for many companies.

Often without warning or explanation, decrees are issued that ban a particular product from importation or pronounce that a particular business activity will no longer be approved for joint ventures. Then, exceptions to the new rules are seen being granted.

New rules are sometimes not communicated to the business community in a timely fashion. For example, an Ernst & Young client newsletter reported recently that the employer's payroll contribution to Vietnam's social insurance fund had been increased from 10% to 15%. The newsletter notes that "although issued on June 22, 1993, Decree 43 CD from the Government is effective from April 1, 1993."

Rules can be different for different people and projects. Conceptually, there is nothing unusual about skewing a tax and licensing code for business to steer investment in the direction in which the government wants it to go. Yet businesspeople are uncomfortable with the lack of transparency of these procedures, believing that too many decisions are made not on the basis of objective criteria and fair play but on the whims or self-interest of bureaucrats and politicians. Preferential tax and land-use rates, how much capital you have to put in and when, and whether you can open an offshore bank account—these are just some of the important issues that more often than not are negotiated with government officials as part of the approval process rather than clearly spelled out in law and regulation. Eugene Matthews points out that "all decisions in Vietnam are collective. There is no silver bullet for success."

Not only is there the usual conflict between the central and local levels of government over economic priorities and the desirability of projects, but bureaucracies also come into conflict within a jurisdiction. The construction of a major office and apartment complex in Hanoi, for example, was stalled because different city agencies squabbled over the height of the building. To their credit, Hanoi city officials have openly acknowledged such problems and have promised to address them.

The *Wall Street Journal* notes that "bureaucrats at all levels wield tremendous power. The danger is that red tape will stifle reform." Others, although not disputing that conclusion, observe that power is diffuse and thus that decision making is excruciatingly slow. Journalist Murray Hiebert quotes an Australian executive's lament that "the downside of doing business is the length of time it takes to get anything done. There's a lot of collective irresponsibility. No one seems to be in a position to make a decision."

Coming face to face with these frustrations has tempted a number of businesspeople to look for shortcuts to circumvent the rules. This is very risky, according to a senior Ho Chi Minh City official who told me that one of the most common mistakes foreign entrepreneurs with local connections make is to have local residents make investments on their behalf unofficially and off the books without submitting to the normal approval process. According to this official, there have been cases

Problems and Pitfalls

in which investors have done that and then are cheated. They have absolutely no legal recourse open to them.

Many of those who register complaints about bureaucracy and red tape also give the Vietnamese credit for being open to advice and improvements. There have reportedly been instances in which Vietnamese officials attending international conferences on business opportunities in their country have gone home afterward seeking to act on the complaints and suggestions they heard.

CORRUPTION

Addressing the extent of corruption facing international business in Vietnam is difficult because of the following:

1. The definition of corrupt versus acceptable behavior differs from culture to culture and person to person.
2. Businesspeople tend to form sweeping judgments on the basis of their personal experience. One who is asked for a bribe tends to brand the whole system as corrupt, whereas one who has never faced it proclaims the system clean.
3. Few who make payments would want to admit it, especially Americans who have the Foreign Corrupt Practices Act to contend with.

There is corruption in Vietnam. The government recognizes it and has launched various "crusades" to clean it up. The press is allowed to report on it, as the *Vietnam Investment Review* did recently in a major articled titled "Construction Industry Fraught with Fraud."

Observers see corruption taking several forms. Given the power they wield, the low pay their receive, and the lucrative deals they see happening all around them, some middle-level bureaucrats cannot resist the temptation to implicitly or explicitly seek payments for expediting and getting projects approved.

As a result of the scarcity of vital business services, it has been reported that many providers expect to be paid to move a request to the top of the list. This form of corruption affects not only foreigners but local residents as well. Murray Heibert reports that "Hanoi residents say it is now virtually impossible to find a job, get a license to build a house, receive treatment in a hospital, get a child into a nursery school, obtain a visa to travel abroad, or secure a business or import-export license without paying bribes." The situation in Ho Chi Minh City, his sources indicated, is just as bad.

Nepotism and flagrant conflicts of interest are also reported, with numerous officials being heavily involved in business activities, some of which were generated by leads and contacts gained on the job. However, not all business cultures brand such conduct as "corruption."

A number of businesspeople I spoke with, including some who have been successful in Vietnam, think that the extent of corruption confronting foreign businesses in Vietnam is overstated. "Paying bribes is a waste of money. Don't do it," one foreign businessman living in Ho Chi Minh City told me. He added that the facet of the bureaucracy people complain about the most—the fact that no one person can ever seem to make a decision—can be a blessing in disguise when it comes to corruption. If you get hit up for a payment when you go through one door, you can always find another door to go through.

A Hong Kong businessman echoes this advice: "If there is a serious form of corruption, it is the corruption that comes from middlemen demanding money to make things happen when in fact they can't deliver. They'll say you can't do it without them, but in fact you can." He adds that by building relationships and making friends first—where, at the most, small gifts are exchanged or a meal is hosted—you are less likely to confront the most flagrant abuses.

Companies should, of course, consult their own legal counsel to determine what is acceptable under laws such as the Foreign Corrupt Practices Act of the United States. The bottom line on corruption, based on my consultations in Vietnam, is this: Don't pay bribes. You can do business successfully without them.

PARTNERS AND THEIR PROMISES

I was advised repeatedly by both executives operating in Vietnam and the consultants who counsel corporate clients that the choice of a Vietnamese business partner, as much as any other single factor, determines whether a venture succeeds or fails.

Hong Kong businessman Paul Ho told me, "Choose your partner very carefully. Watch out for someone who says 'I can get land.' Check it out very thoroughly." *Vietnam Investment Review*'s Ross Dunkley adds, "You are destined to fail if your partner can't carry through on his promises."

In fact, as of March 1994, one of every seven foreign investment licenses granted by the government had expired or was revoked. Often the reason was that one or more of the partners couldn't deliver on their commitments.

Careful research and extensive legwork on the ground in Vietnam is required to find a suitable partner. The State Committee for Cooperation and Investment, the Vietnam Chamber of Commerce and Industry, a service outfit such as the Foreign Investment Service Company, and the local people's committees can help you identify partners. But even when they do, you should cross-check their nominees carefully with other organizations. Don't rely on one referral alone. You may have been steered in a certain direction by those with a financial or political interest that is unknown to you. Eugene Matthews says that one of the most important things a foreign company can do is define its own relationship with the government. "Companies should not solely depend on their local partners to steer projects through the government, particularly in the South. If a problem arises down the line and it is necessary to access people in Hanoi, no one will know you."

Learn from what has worked. Andrew Homan of the *Vietnam Investment Review* has concluded that "the smaller projects with good partners are the ones that seem to be working the best."

THE PHYSICAL AND FINANCIAL INFRASTRUCTURE

Vietnam's inadequate infrastructure makes it difficult and costly to transport goods. Valuable time is wasted attempting to complete simple tasks such as placing phone calls and sending faxes. Frequent power outages in the south cause costly disruptions in business operations.

Despite the admirable Vietnamese commitment to the value of education, skill levels are dropping as a result of shortcomings in the public education program. There is a severe shortage of Western-style management skills in the business, professional, and government sectors.

In the financial area, a shortage of capital and foreign exchange has the potential to choke off growth. Price Waterhouse concludes that

> Vietnam's banking system is still fairly underdeveloped and remains one of the most significant bottlenecks frustrating foreign investors.
>
> Although foreign banks are allowed to grant loans in Vietnam, most foreign banks have so far found it

difficult to obtain financial data from borrowers in order to make sound assessments of their financial position due to a lack of understanding of western accounting practices.

A lack of foreign exchange also creates problems for some investors. A Price Waterhouse analysis summarizes that

> The basic rule is that businesses should be self-sufficient in foreign exchange. In other words, if they need foreign currency to pay expenses, repatriate profits, repay loans and so on, they should be able to generate that currency themselves. They do not have the automatic right to convert Vietnamese dong into foreign currency.

As discussed in an earlier chapter, Vietnam's need for infrastructure affords foreign firms great opportunities. But until those opportunities come to fruition and the infrastructure is improved, roadblocks will remain the rule. And watch out for those 10-foot potholes!

HIGH COSTS AND BURDENSOME TAXES

Despite Vietnam's status as a poor, underdeveloped nation, operating costs are constantly underestimated by businesses entering the market.

Shortages of business necessities such as office space, residences suitable for expatriates, adequately trained staff, communications, and transportation (among others) have driven up prices. So has the emergence of a two-tier pricing structure in which foreigners are charged double or more the local price for some services like electricity.

For example, until recently foreigners were charged $150 for a one-way ticket from Ho Chi Minh City to Hanoi on Vietnam Airlines. The same ticket costs a local Vietnamese $75. After receiving complaints from foreigners about the high cost of the trip, airline officials responded by raising the price for the locals! By 1995, Vietnam Airlines will phase out the two-tier pricing system.

An Australian journalist living in Ho Chi Minh City told me the story of a foreign company that wanted to rent a villa for use as an office and residence for its office manager. The owner wanted $70,000 to pay for renovations, $10,000 a month in rent, and five years' rent in advance! (A more common price for such a facility is reported to be $5,000 a month, with office space generally going for $40 to $50 per square meter in Hanoi and Ho Chi Minh City.)

Although low labor costs are undoubtedly one of Vietnam's major attractions to investors, these too are driven up by the fact that companies are required to hire workers through state recruitment agencies and pay 2% to 3% of the annual salary as commission.

Vietnam is not immune to labor disputes, some of which have been brought about by abusive employers. In early 1994, the *Vietnam Investment Review* reported "a rash of strikes over pay and conditions in Ho Chi Minh City."

The potential tax burden of a foreign company and employee is high:

- Corporations pay a profits tax of 15% to 25%.
- There is a payroll tax of 15% for the social insurance fund.
- Profits repatriated out of Vietnam are subject to an additional tax of 5% to 10%.
- A personal income tax was enacted in 1990 with a top tax rate for foreigners of 50%.
- A turnover tax is levied at different rates on the sale of most goods and services in Vietnam.
- There are fees for leasing land, with the costs depending on location, market conditions, and negotiation.

The potential cumulative effect of these taxes and fees makes it all the more critical to petition government regulators during the licensing process that you should qualify for a range of tax holidays and special incentives earmarked for various investments. Benefits exist for reinvestment of profits. (For a more detailed outline of tax rates and possible incentives for various business activities, see the government-issued regulations in chapter 15 in the Resource Guide.)

Finally, although doing business in Vietnam may not be as cheap as many expect, it can hardly be termed expensive when compared to other major business centers. A businessman in Hanoi estimates that it costs a company about $40,000 a year to keep a westerner in that city, excluding salary. A local staff person for your office—for example, a university graduate who is fluent in English—can be hired for approximately $300 a month. Try accomplishing those feats in Hong Kong, Tokyo, or Singapore!

BACKLASH BACK HOME

Regrettably, one pitfall that concerns some U.S. companies is whether doing business in Vietnam will trigger a consumer or employee backlash back home.

In late 1993, Mobil was criticized by U.S. veterans for holding a reception for Vietnamese officials and oil industry representatives in Reunification Hall in Saigon. The problem for the veterans was that the hall had been the presidential palace of President Nguyen Van Thieu until North Vietnamese tanks crashed through the gates on April 30, 1975. Mobil issued a statement of apology.

American automakers have also been reported (by the *Vietnam Investment Review*) to be moving carefully in exploring Vietnam as a market for fear of angering U.S. consumers. A Chrysler spokesman said, "Certainly it's part of the decision. It's not just a business decision."

The potential for criticism is there. But judging by the number of high-profile visits and entries into the market by major American companies, most have determined that the backlash potential is small and that their reasons for wanting to be in Vietnam are fully defensible.

8

CHALLENGES AND OPPORTUNITIES FOR OVERSEAS VIETNAMESE AND THE COMPANIES WHO HIRE THEM

As U.S. companies were cheering in the hours after President Clinton ended the U.S. trade embargo and an all-night celebration was under way among expatriates in Hanoi, the city of Westminster in Orange County, California, put its police force on alert.

Westminster is otherwise known by its nickname, Little Saigon—home and commercial center to the largest community of Vietnamese outside Vietnam. Police became concerned when a demonstration of several hundred protestors erupted spontaneously after the decision was announced and was shortly followed by several anonymous arson threats directed at prominent Vietnamese-Americans who had advocated an end to the embargo.

Several days later, I attended a ceremony in the heart of Little Saigon in observance of Tet, the Vietnamese lunar new year. It was clear that the president's decision had brought to the surface the deep divisions within the

121

community over the course of U.S. relations with the communist government of Vietnam. Some Vietnamese carried placards that read "Don't Feed the VC" and "Boycott Clinton." Others like Dr. Co Pham, president of the Vietnamese Chamber of Commerce of Orange County, cheered the news. President Clinton "means it as a gift to the Vietnamese people," Pham said. "It is a historic gesture, and though there will be opposition, it may not last for long."

Another local Vietnamese businessman observed, "A lot of people have already been going [to Vietnam] but in a clandestine fashion. The Japanese, the Russians, the Europeans, they all want a piece of the pie. It's only fair that Vietnamese-Americans have the same chance."

ATTITUDES OF OVERSEAS VIETNAMESE ARE CHANGING

Despite some flashes of anger and protest, most observers felt the reaction was more muted than expected. As one whose political and governmental assignments have brought me into contact for many years with the Vietnamese community in California, I have observed a dramatic softening in attitude among the community known as *Viet Kieu* (pronounced "viet cue": "overseas Vietnamese") toward relations with their homeland. In fact, a June 1994 Los Angeles Times poll of the community in southern California found that 54% supported not only the lifting of the embargo but also the establishment of full diplomatic relations.

(Note: I have met a few Vietnamese who don't like the label *Viet Kieu*, believing it is somehow a manipulation by the Hanoi government to trap them in a kind of no-man's land between being a "real" Vietnamese and a "real" citizen of their new country. These individuals

prefer being referred to as Vietnamese, Vietnamese-Americans, or simply Americans.)
A number of factors explain the shift.

Family Visits

No one would have predicted 10 years ago that Vietnamese-Americans, including those who had been imprisoned in "reeducation camps" and escaped by sea, would now be making routine visits back home to visit their loved ones. Allowing these visits beginning in the late 1980s was the smartest thing the Vietnamese government could have done to influence the attitudes of the *Viet Kieu* toward their homeland.

Hundreds of thousands have returned for one or more visits. In 1993 alone, 28% of Vietnam's 700,000 foreign visitors were overseas Vietnamese. Given the paramount importance of family, Vietnamese do not want to risk any "refreezing" of relations that would interfere with these reunions.

The Passage of Time and the Ascension of a New Generation

It has been 20 years since the fall of Saigon. The old warriors among the original group of refugees are fading while a new generation who did all or most of their growing up in America are assuming leadership posts in the community. Although they are deferential to the views of their more conservative parents, these Vietnamese-Americans are emotionally distant from past battles and more concerned with the future and practical considerations.

It was reported that a high school teacher discussing the end of the embargo with her mainly Vietnamese students posed the question, "What do you think will be the biggest impact of the end of the embargo on the two countries?" The students rather blandly answered that it would be easier to visit Vietnam because U.S. airlines would be able to fly there now!

Economic Decline in the United States and the Ascension of Southeast Asia

The Vietnamese community in California has been hit hard by the economic contradictions of the late 1980s and early 1990s, particularly by layoffs in the defense and electronics industries. This in turn has affected the small retail businesses on which many other Vietnamese rely for their livelihoods.

At the same time, many are tantalized by reports of booming business opportunities in their native land. Many Vietnamese, particularly younger college-educated Vietnamese, sense that their moment has finally arrived—that by virtue of their background they have a special set of skills and unique knowledge that will be in great demand.

Love of Country

Many Vietnamese found visiting their homeland a shocking experience because of the extensive poverty and dilapidated state of their old neighborhoods. They feel a strong impulse to aid in the reconstruction of Vietnam despite the presence of what they consider an unfriendly government. They have concluded that the continued isolation of Vietnam will mean only continued poverty.

There are an estimated 400,000 Vietnamese living in California and over 800,000 living in the United States as well as sizable communities in Canada, Australia, and France. Despite the factors that have brought them closer to their homeland, these concentrations of Vietnamese maintain many of the trappings of an "exile" community.

A daily television newscast in southern California begins each day by playing the South Vietnamese national anthem. The South Vietnamese flag hangs in the homes of many Vietnamese-Americans. Although talk of "retaking the country" is less overt now, it still exists. Conservatives in control of most of the Vietnamese-language news media give the impression that the community as a whole is more opposed to relations with Vietnam than is really the case. The loudest voices are the ones arguing most strenuously for isolating Vietnam. Those wanting to build bridges have been reluctant to come forward. Some are afraid to do so.

Attitudes of the Vietnamese Government

If attitudes among *Viet Kieu* are divided but softening, the attitudes and approaches of the Vietnamese government toward them are decidedly ambivalent.

The government's explicit policy is to welcome *Viet Kieu* and urge their participation in the development of the country. Its official story on why so many have chosen to flee their homeland is, if nothing else, revealing. As one official explained to me, the ones who left got caught up on the wrong side of the country's thousand-year struggle for independence. Under normal circumstances, they would be standing shoulder to shoulder with their countrymen, but for a variety of reasons they ended up on the wrong side of their country's historic struggle. On reflection and with the passage of time, they will rejoin the struggle to keep Vietnam free of foreign domination. Repeatedly, officials I have met with in government agencies and Vietnamese business organizations in Hanoi and

Da Nang as well as in Ho Chi Minh City have emphasized that they want to receive *Viet Kieu* delegations from the United States to explore business opportunities. In mid-1994, *Viet Kieu* staying in the major Saigon hotels were given a five-page government questionnaire exploring their attitudes about the country's business climate for overseas Vietnamese.

In an even more overt effort to court overseas Vietnamese, in 1993 the Vietnamese prime minister decreed preferential tax treatment for *Viet Kieu* investors, cutting the 10% tax on profits charged to other foreigners to 5%.

As of 1993, just 30 of the nearly 900 licensed foreign investment projects belonged to overseas Vietnamese. But this masks the increasingly important economic role the community plays in its homeland. Relatives still living in Vietnam are frequently used as "fronts" for off-the-books investments by overseas Vietnamese. The infusion of hard currency into the economy by hundreds of thousands of *Viet Kieu* tourists cannot be overstated. And the government is certainly pleased to have the estimated $1 billion that *Viet Kieu* send to their relatives each year, money that basically funds a social welfare system in Ho Chi Minh City free of charge.

Yet the fact remains that Vietnamese authorities still harbor a deep distrust of the overseas Vietnamese community as a whole. Manifestations of the community's exile status, such as displaying the South Vietnamese flag and playing its national anthem, are anathema to the governing regime—proof positive, in its eyes, of the existence of an enemy force plotting to do it harm.

Until recently, a question written only in Vietnamese on the foreigner's application for a Vietnam visa asked pointedly, "What did you do in Vietnam before 1975?" I have seen visiting Vietnamese questioned far more thoroughly and pointedly by customs and immigration authorities on their way in and out of the country. Many Vietnamese in America are convinced that the government is keeping tabs on them and their activities in the United States through a network of sympathetic informants, although no one has proved this.

Negotiations between the United States and Vietnam over the opening of liaison offices and the establishment of diplomatic ties were stalled for a time, further revealing the sensitivity of the Hanoi government to overseas Vietnamese in their country. Hanoi reportedly wanted to recognize Vietnamese with American passports not as Americans but as Vietnamese! This would have denied Vietnamese-Americans the same protections afforded other foreign passport holders. Washington held firm, and the issue is now considered resolved, at least in theory.

CONSIDERATIONS FOR COMPANIES HIRING OVERSEAS VIETNAMESE

Given the complex relationship and cloudy atmosphere that exists between the Vietnamese homeland and the overseas community, what considerations should come into play for companies considering hiring Vietnamese to represent their interests? This frequently asked question is a touchy one. Many businesspeople and consultants do not want to be quoted on the record.

One foreigner doing business in Vietnam told me bluntly, "The local Vietnamese hate the *Viet Kieu*. They believe they abandoned the country for the good life in the West and now they are coming back flashing money and showing off."

Another consultant told me, "Don't hire *Viet Kieu* to represent you in Vietnam. They are not trusted." She recounted a story in which a well-known firm had its license delayed for months, the only reason to which those familiar with the application could point being that the proposal included a *Viet Kieu* to run the office. Another businessman who set up a hotel in Saigon refined this advice, saying that although naming an overseas Vietnamese as the top person in your local office could be trouble, it could be very helpful to have such a person in your number two position.

A French executive based in Hanoi was quoted recently in *Fortune* magazine:

> We think there is a lot of risk in hiring a *Viet Kieu*. You have to know what his parents did before 1975, who they were close to, who they crossed. Yet knowing someone's past is not enough, because you can never be sure how the authorities will interpret his past. A bad *Viet Kieu* can do you a lot of harm, whereas a bad Frenchman, well, you just send him back to France.

Vietnamese-Americans I have spoken to are hurt by this kind of talk making the rounds in international business circles. In fact, there are individuals with Vietnamese backgrounds who are successfully operating representative offices for major companies (such as Bank of America's Luu Le). Chinese-Vietnamese from Hong Kong and Singapore are handling many important projects on behalf of their companies. Vietnamese-Americans are also successfully providing consulting and other professional services for U.S. businesses.

Yet the talk is out there, and the issue is of serious concern. As a businessperson, only you can determine how best to live up to your own sense of morality in making hiring decisions (not to mention applicable laws governing discrimination in hiring). My purpose is to advise you that this is an issue.

Here are the considerations that come into play when hiring a *Viet Kieu:*

1. An individual of Vietnamese background can play an invaluable role, given his or her knowledge of the culture, language, business practices, and market mechanisms, accomplishing tasks in a

fraction of the time it would take a non-Vietnamese. A *Viet Kieu* will likely be highly motivated to perform well, given that the work is related to the economic progress of his or her homeland.

2. At the same time, the individual's language and cultural skills may be dated. Most have spent the greater part of their adult lives outside Vietnam and have never had to operate professionally under either communism or *doi moi*. Some returning Vietnamese have even noticed a slight language barrier after a 15-plus-years absence, with new words, usages, and expressions having been introduced since they left. Note also that a difference does exist between the Northern and Southern dialects.

3. Check the family and political backgrounds of your *Viet Kieu* applicant thoroughly, not necessarily to find something disqualifying but simply to know what roadblocks you might face. Chances are that if the individual's family was highly connected to the former South Vietnamese government or has been active and visible in antigovernment activities in the United States, he or she would not be seeking to return to Vietnam anyway. If so, maybe you *should* question motives and expediency!

4. Beware of Vietnamese claiming that you should hire them because "I know so many people in Vietnam and have so many good connections." In their eagerness to prove their worth, some *Viet Kieu* exaggerate their current influence back home. The reputation of *Viet Kieu* entrepreneurs was unfairly tainted early on by the appearance of the so-called cowboys, a small number of slick operators who went to Vietnam and made some

big promises about the barrels of investment capital they could deliver. They never did.

5. Don't overlook the fact that the pull of family for some Vietnamese could cloud their business decisions. There is a sometimes irresistible temptation to swing business in the direction of relatives or to make hiring decisions on the basis of family loyalties rather than sound business practices. Loyalty to family is one of the most attractive qualities of the Vietnamese. In some cases, however, it can cloud sound judgment.

CONSIDERATIONS FOR OVERSEAS VIETNAMESE

Viet Kieu responding to the opening of Vietnam will want to ask, "Do I have a special opportunity to become involved in the rebuilding of my country? A special handicap? Does my Vietnamese background help me or hurt me?"

Balancing all factors, I am convinced that there are many avenues of opportunity open for those with a Vietnamese background.

Although as a *Viet Kieu* you will be spared some of the problems that non-Vietnamese face when doing business in Vietnam, you may confront some or all of a different set of challenges: a higher degree of suspicion and scrutiny by authorities, rebuffs by companies who have made a blanket decision not to hire *Viet Kieu,* criticism from fellow Vietnamese in both your old country and your new one, and even criticism from family members. As those who have returned after many years of absence know full well, you will have to reacquaint yourself with your own culture and language. In the poignant words of one returnee trying to do business in Vietnam, "The most difficult thing was the feeling of loneliness. It's your country and you feel like a stranger."

When approaching companies and businesspeople you would like to join, conduct yourself with professionalism and seriousness, not flamboyance. Emphasize your business skills equally with your language and cultural knowledge. Remember, companies are alert to exaggerated claims of close connections in Vietnam. Don't overstate your case. Be forthright if you believe there are any questions to be raised about your family background.

Also, look to the examples of others to see who has been successful and who has not. One *Viet Kieu* managing a major hotel in Saigon was quoted recently as saying, "I saw a few *Viet Kieu* guys come here, representing big companies, big mouths, they're in trouble."

Yet there are many success stories among former refugees, including these:

- Giang Tran of San Diego formed the Vietnam Investment Information and Consulting firm, which organized the April 1994 Vietnamerica Expo, which displayed American products and services in Hanoi.

- Victor Duong began a company in Oakland, California, in 1982 whose "inventory" consisted of discarded paper on the streets that his company retrieved for recycling. From there, he moved into environmental technologies and has just received a contract from the city of Hai Phong to help set up garbage disposal and recycling services there.

- Nguyen Trung Truc left Vietnam in 1972 and returned in 1989. After a few false starts in business, he formed a joint venture with Hong Kong–based Peregrine Capital Limited. Today, as reported by the *Far Eastern Economic Review,* Mr. Truc "runs a wide-ranging business network involved in distribution and marketing, property development and banking." His firm represents Johnson & Johnson baby care products in Vietnam as well as Kenwood electronics and Mercedes Benz cars.

Many other overseas Vietnamese are being tapped to work in Hong Kong's or Singapore's regional headquarters of big manufacturing companies and consumer products, accounting, and consulting firms, all to help guide corporate strategies in Vietnam.

In the words of economic analyst Joel Kotkin, "After 20 years, Vietnam's wayward children could end up with front-row seats in the development of a new and powerful Asian economy."

OPPORTUNITIES FOR OVERSEAS VIETNAMESE

If you are a Vietnamese living in the United States, Canada, Australia, or some other location, how can you participate in the opportunities that await businesspeople in Vietnam? There are several strategies open to you.

1. *Investing and trading.* Should you be in a position to invest in or trade with the country, pursue the strategies detailed in the earlier chapters of this book. Use your special knowledge of the people, language, culture, and marketplace as an advantage to help you move more quickly than your competitors. *Don't* use these attributes as crutches in place of doing your homework or making decisions on the basis of good business rather than sentimentality. Take care to follow the established procedures, for you will be scrutinized more closely and thus are more likely to be caught breaking the rules than your non-Vietnamese counterparts.

2. *Multinational corporations.* Unless through your educational background and work experience you have been grooming yourself for a career in corporate America, do not expect its doors to

open to you simply because you are Vietnamese. If you believe you have the background and résumé to be competitive, send letters with your résumé to the international divisions and marketing departments of companies you know are interested in expanding into Vietnam. Become active in the organizations listed in chapter 12 in the Resource Guide to build your contact base and collect job leads.

3. *Services, information, and consulting.* A greater range of opportunities exists for those able to provide the many companies, trade associations, and law, accounting, architectural, and urban planning firms with specialized services for their Vietnam-related projects. These concerns need language skills, document translation, bilingual staffing at trade fairs, and account executives who can bridge the gaps between both cultures.

Study the market carefully and monitor closely the various projects under way. When a company is involved in a major construction project, public relations contract, or architectural or hotel project, there may be a role for you to play, at least temporarily. Keep a close watch on activities in Vietnam that are related to your profession. Then market yourself on the basis of both your professional skills and your Vietnamese background.

You can contact the companies directly or attempt to attach yourself to one of the consulting firms whose business it is to secure these kinds of clients. Consider also the diverse opportunities in the tourist industry as well as the new multiplier groups springing up, such as Vietnam-related chambers of commerce and trade associations.

Some of these opportunities, especially in the area of consulting, may result in only temporary assignments. But through them you can compile a track record and perhaps catch the eye of a major corporate client who will offer you a position with greater long-term potential.

Creating prosperity for yourself and your family in the new Vietnam will not be any easier than it was to create a new life for yourself overseas. But you and your families did it before under great duress. You can do it again, this time under more favorable and constructive conditions. Even in the face of special challenges, great opportunities await you in Vietnam, and you have a chance to play a vital role in the expansion of commercial and friendship ties between the United States and Vietnam. It will take patience, hard work, and careful nurturing, but in the words of the Vietnamese proverb, *Nang am cay moi xanh!* (pronounced "nang ahm kay moy sun": "The warm sun will bring the green tree!").

Part Two
The Doing Business
in Vietnam Resource Guide

9

GUIDE TO BUSINESS TRAVEL IN VIETNAM

It is hoped that the first section of this book has convinced you to go to Vietnam, to see the country, and to assess your opportunities. You may return convinced that this emerging market is right for your company, or you may decide that this is not the time and Vietnam not the place. Whatever the case, I can assure you that Vietnam will be a travel experience you won't forget. Americans in particular would have to be blind to history not to be profoundly affected when visiting a country and a people that have figured so emotionally in our national psyche.

The purpose of this section is to tell you what you need to know to conduct your exploratory business trip and activities in Vietnam. In the course of trying to leave as few questions as possible unanswered, I may make the process sound more complicated than it really is. It *is* more complicated than traveling to many other countries, but don't be intimidated. Hundreds of thousands of business travelers and tourists are now making the trip, either in groups or on their own, and for most it is a rewarding, trouble-free experience!

BEFORE YOU GO

Visas

All visitors entering Vietnam, for whatever reason, are required to possess valid passports and visas. The process of securing a visa is cumbersome for Americans because they have no diplomatic relations with Vietnam and thus no Vietnamese embassies and consular offices here. As this book is being published, the two countries have agreed to establish liaison offices in each other's capital. It is unclear when these offices will be equipped to issue visas.

The two most common types of visas are the tourist visa and the business visa. Even though the tourist visa is meant for sightseers only, many business travelers utilize the tourist visa for those early exploratory trips. They don't plan to conduct actual business transactions and don't even know yet whether they will. Recently, the authorities have put out the word that they are imposing fines on those they discover entering the country on a tourist visa when they are really there for business. Yet, realistically, if you are visiting Vietnam to look around, have a few exploratory meetings, and assess the market, you will not be questioned. Even if you are, you could legitimately state that the trip falls more into the category of tourism rather than business at those early stages.

Why is this an issue? Because getting a tourist visa is a relatively simple process, whereas securing a business visa is not.

To arrange a tourist visa, contact your travel agent. Allow at least three weeks if you reside in the United States because your travel agent must work through Vietnamese embassy officials in either Mexico or Canada. You will fill out a form and then submit a copy of your passport and two passport-sized photos. Travel agents usually charge anywhere from $50 to $80 for this service. If your travel agent is unfamiliar with the process, he or she should be able to find another who can perform this service. You can't go wrong with travel agencies that cater to the Vietnamese-American community. They have this process down pat, having done it for hundreds if not thousands of compatriots going home for family visits.

Your visa will be dated and good for one month. It is not stamped in your passport but rather is issued as a separate document.

Residents of countries with diplomatic relations with Vietnam should contact the nearest Vietnamese embassy or consulate.

Securing a business visa requires a Vietnamese "sponsor," such as the Vietnam Chamber of Commerce and Industry, the Foreign Investment Service Company, a government ministry, or a local people's committee. Utilize the fax numbers contained in chapter 12 in the Resource Guide to apply for your visa. If you are organizing a high-profile business delegation, this is the way to go. There are charges for the visa service, and the entity you contact will most likely want to put a program together for you, again for a charge.

One other option for securing a visa is available if you are planning a stopover in Asia before the final leg of your trip to Vietnam. Visas can be arranged in Bangkok, Singapore, and Hong Kong, where a special office has been opened for this purpose. The timeliness with which embassies can make arrangements varies. Also, there are weekends and both local and Vietnamese holidays to contend with, so unless your stopover is at least five business days, it is better to have the whole process taken care of before you leave home. Under no circumstances should you arrive in Vietnam without a visa.

How to Get There

Currently, no American-flag carrier flies all the way into Vietnam, although several are primed and ready to go once they receive permission from various authorities. If you fly an American-flag carrier to Asia, you must (1) stop for at least one night elsewhere in Southeast Asia because of flight schedules and (2) book your actual flight in and out of Vietnam on another carrier. Most travelers from North America stop in Hong Kong, Bangkok, or Singapore; recover from jet lag and perhaps make some Vietnam-related contacts; and then fly into Ho Chi Minh City on Cathay Pacific, Thai, or Singapore airlines.

Several airlines offer an uninterrupted (and very long) journey from the West Coast of the United States to Vietnam without an overnight layover, including Philippine, China, and Singapore airlines.

Be sure to book your flights well in advance, particularly the portion getting you in and out of Vietnam, as they are often fully booked. If you are planning to visit Vietnam any time during or near the Vietnamese new year (Tet) in late January to early February and haven't booked flights and hotels months in advance, forget it!

Hotel Reservations

Because of the paucity of hotels in Vietnam, especially Hanoi, you should not arrive in Vietnam without an advance booking. That's easier said than done.

Most hotels are unfamiliar with the process of having a customer call or fax to guarantee a room reservation with a credit card. Even professional travel agents have no formalized relationships with hotels in Vietnam. Rather, they must rely on an informal network of contacts and relatives in the country to make bookings and leave deposits on behalf of their clients.

This situation is likely to change quickly. In the space of less than two years, I watched most of the major hotels in Ho Chi Minh City move from handwritten ledgers and record keeping to computerized reservations and account systems. With credit cards now gaining acceptance in Vietnam and alliances being formed between hotels and the U.S. travel industry, the process of securing lodging will soon be more convenient.

For now, here are your options:

1. Utilize a travel agent with contacts in Vietnam who can book you a room. Be sure to get a written receipt for your booking and for any deposit that has been left at your hotel on your behalf. Despite the introduction of computers, many Vietnamese still trust that little piece of paper more.

2. If you are working through an organization such as the Vietnam Chamber of Commerce and Industry, the Foreign Investment Service Company, or any other substantial Vietnamese organization to set up your business program and visa, also ask them to book rooms for you.

3. Send a fax to Saigontourist, Ho Chi Minh City's leading tour company (a government entity that happens to own many of the hotels) and ask them to book your rooms throughout the country as well as ground-travel arrangements and tours. This has worked well for me in the past. They will respond with a faxed confirmation. The only complicating factor is that you must go to the Saigontourist office before checking into your hotel to pay your bill and get your vouchers. If your flight arrives late in the evening, this approach may not work! Saigontourist is conveniently located at 49 Le Thanh Ton Street, District 1, Ho Chi Minh City (tel: 84-8-230-102; fax: 84-8-224-987).

Recently, many smaller guest houses and minihotels have sprung up in both Ho Chi Minh City and Hanoi, so it is possible that if you arrive in Vietnam without a hotel reservation, your cab driver can find you one. Yet, for the business traveler these facilities can be inconveniently located and lack necessary communications and other services. (We'll discuss specific hotels and their services after we "arrive" in Vietnam!)

What to Pack, What to Bring, and the Color of Your Money

Although winter in Hanoi requires wearing a sweater and light overcoat, Vietnam's climate is basically tropical, hot, and humid. Pack accordingly, depending on your schedule and purpose of the trip. (For pointers on how to dress for business meetings, see chapter 6.) Laundry service, even at hotels, is cheaper than it is at your local cleaners. In addition, be sure to bring the following:

- At least two extra passport photos. Visa notwithstanding, you will need one right at the airport when you arrive!
- Plenty of business cards. Take what you think you'll need and then double it!
- Plenty of U.S. dollars in all denominations. This is important. In one of the strange ironies of postwar Vietnam, the U.S. dollar has long been the currency of choice in Vietnam, even at the height of the trade embargo. Some locations, such as hotels, may even refuse to take their country's own currency, demanding dollars instead!

Furthermore, although the situation is changing fast, do not count on being able to use your credit cards or traveler checks in Vietnam. Be sure to have enough cash to pay for accommodations and other potentially high-cost items such as plane tickets from Ho Chi Minh City to Hanoi.

Take a variety of small bills for paying taxis and other services that you might have negotiated in dollars. Most service establishments will give you prices in both currencies (the exchange rate is about one U.S. dollar for 10,700 dong), but dollars are preferred. Expect small change back in dong. Do not expect a taxi driver, for example, to be able to change your hundred- or even twenty-dollar bill. So keep a stash of ones, fives, and tens with you as well. Non-U.S. residents should be sure to change a sufficient amount of their own currency into U.S. dollars before embarking on their trip.

Dollars are difficult if not impossible to obtain once in Vietnam. It is a good idea to change some money into dong to use for smaller purchases, cyclos, and other needs. Just be sure to use it all before you get to the airport because you will not be able to change it back!

Arriving in Vietnam

Immigration and Customs

As your flight approaches either Noi Bai Airport in Hanoi or Tan Son Nhut Airport in Ho Chi Minh City, the flight attendant will likely advise you that for security reasons the Vietnamese government prohibits taking photographs from the airplane's window before landing and on the airport's tarmac. No explanation is offered.

Remember the visa you went to the expense and trouble of securing back home? You get to spend about half of the last, short leg of your trip filling out the forms all over again. The flight attendant will give you (1) an application for entry and exit to Vietnam for foreigners (you must have an extra passport photo to submit with this form), (2) an entry/exit card, and (3) two copies of a customs declaration form to be filled out identically.

Customs is the most cumbersome part of the process of entering and exiting Vietnam. You must include on your form personal effects such as your watch, wedding ring and other jewelry, camera, and portable stereo as well as cigarettes, alcohol, and the precise amount of currency you are carrying into the country!

Except for customs, the process for entering Vietnam where most visitors do (Tan Son Nhut Airport) has improved greatly over the last year. The arrival hall has been refurbished and air conditioned, and lines, although long and slow, are more orderly. Yet, once you clear immigration and collect your luggage, you just wait in another slow, cumbersome line to clear customs. Excruciatingly slow agents inspect your form and x-ray your belongings. After checking your form, the agent scribbles on it, using a piece of carbon paper to make another copy. He or she then gets up from the desk, walks clear to the other side of the room to an office, and disappears for a couple of minutes. Following a leisurely return, you are led through the gate.

The purpose of this procedure is believed to be to stop *Viet Kieu* from bringing money in, investing it unofficially through family members, and then sneaking the proceeds out of the country to escape taxation. Officials are also concerned about precious family heirlooms making their way out of Vietnam, thus reducing the overall wealth of the country over time. I have seen customs officials pull out a jeweler's eyepiece and other measuring instruments to examine diamond and gold jewelry being worn into the country for fear it is fake and will be replaced with the real thing as the individual leaves the country.

In response to complaints, tourism and other officials have reportedly sought improvements in this hassle, but even commands from higher authorities have failed to improve it much. Just relax, enjoy the show, and perhaps contemplate the well-known Vietnamese proverb: *Phep vua thua le lang!* (pronounced "fep vooa tooa lay lang": "Even the king's command is beaten by the small village rule!").

Authorities don't care how much money you bring into the country as long as the amount of cash you bring out is less. Whatever you do, don't lose your copy of your customs declaration form. It will be scrutinized carefully on your way out of Vietnam.

Airport Transfers

Tan Son Nhut is one of those dying breeds of international airports that is just minutes from the city's center (approximately 7 kilometers, or 4 miles). As you leave the terminal, avoid the hawkers and their private cars and catch a white metered Airport Taxi. The meter starts at 80 cents (down from $2.00 now that two cab companies are competing for your business—ah, the joys of capitalism!). The ride into town takes about 15 minutes and costs just under $7.

Unfortunately, Hanoi's Noi Bai Airport is 35 kilometers, (or 22 miles) from town, and the condition of the road for much of the way is poor. Mostly private cars and minivans without meters are waiting on your arrival. Rides cost anywhere from $15 to $30, depending on your bargaining skills and the desperation of the drivers as the crowd of arriving passengers starts to dwindle.

Hotel Considerations

The quality and level of service at hotels in Ho Chi Minh City has improved greatly in the last two years, as has the number of services provided. Expect clean, comfortable rooms and plentiful service, but don't expect the standards you find in other international business capitals. It's mainly a lack of training, not a lack of trying.

Don't expect great bargains, either. Prices, always stated and payable in U.S. dollars, have been pegged to the foreigners who stay in them.

Status symbols are important in Vietnam, and should you be planning meetings with government officials and industry leaders, you will want to say in one of the "name" hotels.

The better hotels now have international direct-dial telephones, business centers, minibars, air conditioning, television with CNN and other satellite programming, and amenities such as toothbrushes and shampoo. Because of low wage rates and an abundant supply of labor, service in hotels is plentiful but not always well trained. (Lapses, mostly minor, that I have observed include no eye contact from the front-desk clerks and no thank-yous on checking out, chambermaids who in the middle of cleaning your room leave for another part of the hotel to retrieve something and leave your door wide open, and forgotten or mistaken phone messages while you are out.)

One bonus at a number of hotels is the European-style buffet breakfast included in the price of a room.

Of the many hotels I have stayed in, some are dilapidated, but the rooms have always been clean. Bugs and mosquitoes can be a problem, though. Some of the older hotels are equipped with mosquito nets.

One further tip for light sleepers. The cities of Vietnam are noisy places with construction everywhere and much of the living done right on the streets. It is also an "early" society. Unlike cosmopolitan, big-city life in New York, Hong Kong, or Tokyo, people are up and going at the crack of dawn. By 5:30 or 6:00 A.M., you will hear the incessant honking of horns and the racket of jackhammers and pile drivers. So when checking into my hotel, I forgo the "view" and ask for rooms facing inside and away from the street. They are a lot quieter and may even be cheaper.

Here is a selection of Western-style hotels in the two principal business centers of the country, with nondiscounted prices for the largest category of room. These hotels can be booked through Saigontourist, your travel agent, or in some cases directly. In pure status terms, *the* places to stay in Saigon are the Saigon Floating Hotel (which literally sits atop a barge on the Saigon River), the Continental (sedate but full of charm and history), the Rex (a favorite of Americans), the Century Saigon, and the Omni Saigon (first class but unlike the others closer to the airport than to the city's center). At publication time, several other first-class hotels were under construction and scheduled to open soon.

In Hanoi, the choices are more limited. The premier hotel (with premier prices to match) is the Pullman Metropole. International business life centers around that hotel, especially its bar and restaurant. Other deluxe hotels are the Saigon, the Thang Li, and the Hanoi.

For hotels in Da Nang and other cities, work with Saigontourist, Vietnamtourism, or your hotel on arrival in either Ho Chi Minh City or Hanoi.

Hotels in Saigon

Saigon Floating Hotel
Me Linh Square, District 1
Tel: 84-8-290-783
Fax: 84-8-290-784
$224

Century Saigon
68A Nguyen Hue, District 1

Tel: 84-8-293-168
Fax: 84-8-292-732
$121

Rex (Ben Thanh)
141 Nguyen Hue, District 1
Tel: 84-8-296-046
Fax: 84-8-291-469
$82

Continental
132 Dong Khoi Street,
   District 1
Tel: 84-8-299-201
Fax: 84-8-290-936
$99 (breakfast included)

Omni Saigon
251 Nguyen Van Troi,
 Phu Nhuan District
Tel: 84-8-449-222
Fax: 84-8-449-200
$161

Norfolk
117 Le Thanh Ton,
 District 1
Tel: 84-8-295-368
Fax: 84-8-293-415
$86 (breakfast included)

Majestic (Cuu Long)
1 Dong Khoi Street,
 District 1
Tel: 84-8-295-515
Fax: 84-8-291-470
$45 (breakfast included)

Bong Sen
117–119 Dong Khoi Street,
 District 1
Tel: 84-8-291-516
Fax: 84-8-299-744
$49 (breakfast included)

Mondial
109 Dong Khoi Street,
 District 1
Tel:84-8-296-291
Fax: 84-8-296-324
$60

Kim Do
133 Nguyen Hue, District 1
Tel: 84-8-225-914
Fax: 84-8-225-913
$130

Metropole
148 Tran Hung Dao,
 District 1
Tel: 84-8-322-021
Fax: 84-8-322-019
$86 (breakfast included)

Palace Hotel (Huu Nghi)
56–64 Nguyen Hue,
 District 1
Tel: 84-8-292-860
Fax: 84-8-299-872
$60 (breakfast included)

Saigon Star
204 Xo Viet Nghe Tinh,
 District 3
Tel: 84-8-230-260
Fax: 84-8-230-255
$102

Asian Hotel
146–150 Dong Khoi
 Street, District 1
Tel: 84-8-296-979
Fax: 84-8-297-433
$55 (breakfast included)

Hotels in Hanoi

Pullman Metropole
15 Ngo Quyen Street
Tel: 84-4-266-919

Saigon
80 Ly Thuong Kiet Street
Tel: 84-4-268-501

Fax: 84-4-266-920
$182

Thang Loi
Yen Phu Street
Tel: 84-4-268-211
Fax: 84-4-252-800
$71 (breakfast included)

Government Guesthouse
2 Le Thach Street
Tel: 84-4-255-801
Fax: 84-4-259-227
$49

Hoa Binh II
4 Pham Su Manh Street
Tel: 84-4-253-221
Fax: 84-4-269-818
$44 (breakfast included)

Fax: 84-4-266-631
$97 (breakfast included)

Hoa Binh
27 Ly Thuong Kiet Street
Tel: 84-4-253-315
Fax: 84-4-269-818
$45 (breakfast included)

Army Guesthouse I
33A Pham Ngu Lao
Tel: 84-4-255-801
Fax: 84-4-265-539
$44 (breakfast included)

Hanoi
8 Giang Vo Street
Tel: 84-4-252-240
Fax: 84-4-259-209
$179 (breakfast included)

Getting Around

There are three ways to get from place to place and appointment to appointment locally:

1. *Air-conditioned meter taxi.* There are two companies in Saigon, Vinataxi (yellow) and Airport Taxi (white), and one in Hanoi called Hanoi Taxi. Hail cabs outside your hotel or ask the front-desk clerk or the office you are visiting to call one. Meters start at 80 cents in Saigon and $2.00 in Hanoi. Fares are calculated in dollars but are payable in either dollars or dong.

2. *Hired car or minivan.* Compared to other business capitals, hiring your own car and driver for short and long distances is cheap. If you have a busy schedule of meetings, this is the way to go.

Ask your hotel to arrange it, or negotiate on your own the drivers milling around outside your hotel. You should be able to arrange a car and driver for the entire day for $30 to $50.

3. *Cyclos.* These human-powered three-wheeled rickshaws offend the sensibilities of some, but to Vietnamese they provide a perfectly respectable way for passengers to get around and for the pedalers to make a living. Use a cyclo for short–distance trips in good weather. A bonus is that riding in a cyclo is the best way to observe the city and the marketplace up close and personal. Most cyclo drivers working the city's center speak some English and can answer your questions on the way.

Always negotiate the price in advance. For a one-way trip within the central district, drivers usually ask for $2.00, or 20,000 dong. Smile, shake your head, and offer $1.00, and you will usually have a deal. Once at your destination, the driver will want to wait to take you back. Agree for the same price but do not pay him for waiting, as cyclos are plentiful and easy to hail.

For out-of-town business trips, such as a journey from Saigon to Vung Tau or from Hanoi to Hai Phong, the best approach is to hire a car or minivan with a driver.

Vietnam Airlines offers domestic flights throughout the country, including jet service on the Ho Chi Minh–Da Nang–Hanoi route. Some travelers are leery of the aging Russian-built aircraft. Although the service is not up to the standards to which most foreigners are accustomed, the flights I have made have always been punctual. The one-way fire between Hanoi and Ho Chi Ming City is $150. I have never had trouble booking the flights I wanted at the nearest Vietnam Airlines ticket office after my arrival in the country.

Safety on the Streets

Violent street crime is extremely rare in Vietnam, yet pickpocketing is now a serious problem, especially in the business and tourist areas of Saigon. Guard your possessions closely at all times, and don't allow yourself to be distracted by a vendor or a beggar. It could be a setup for a partner in crime approaching from a different angle to "bump" into you. Don't rely on your preconceived notions of what a pickpocket should look like. I have had both young schoolgirls on bicycles and old women in the traditional Vietnamese hats try to rob me!

Walking in the central areas can also be spoiled by the constant approaches of shoeshine boys, stamp and coin album hawkers, and hideously deformed beggars. You may feel compelled to patronize or contribute to one. Just remember that if you do, you will be deluged on the spot by several more. If you want to make your way quickly through the entourage, just stare straight ahead and keep walking.

Business Services

The major hotels offer an adequate range of business services: faxing, photocopying, secretarial services, conference facilities, and word processing. Charges, although not cheap, are considerably less than what you pay in the top hotels in cities like Hong Kong, Bangkok, and Singapore.

Copies are generally 20 cents per page. A one-page fax to the United States is about $10. You can also find slightly cheaper photocopying services on the street, as a number of jewelry shops and grocery stores have invested in copy machines. You can save perhaps a couple of dollars per fax by utilizing the service at the central post offices in Saigon and Hanoi, although you have to balance these savings against the extra time and hassle of going there and pushing and shoving in lines.

Because of the extreme shortage of office space and Western-style residences, many foreigners work out of hotels and utilize these services for weeks and even months. If you plan to stay for an extended period, befriend the hotel manager and discuss a special rate.

Several business service centers are emerging in the business districts of Saigon and Hanoi, but it remains to be seen whether the costs of using these centers will be competitive in price and convenience with what you can accomplish at your hotel. Unless you need actual office space on an ongoing basis, your hotel should be adequate.

Language and Communication

Most of the Vietnamese who the international businessperson encounters in meetings and the major service establishments in the big cities speak just enough English for you to be able to communicate—with patience! Attending English school has become something of a new craze in Saigon and Hanoi among the professional classes, so communication is likely to improve greatly in the near future.

The businessperson's potential to understand Vietnamese is aided by the fact that the language uses a romanized alphabet, not characters or a unique script like Chinese, Japanese, Korean, or Thai. An observant person will quickly be able to associate the most commonly used words on street signs, storefronts, and the like with their meanings.

Telephone Service

The major hotels now have international direct-dial telephones. A three-minute call to the United States will cost $10 to $15. Local calls from your hotel typically cost 20 cents per call.

Vietnam's country code is 84. Each city also has a city code, which must be dialed first if you are calling long distance within the country. Some key city codes are as follows:

- Hanoi: 42
- Ho Chi Minh City: 8
- Hai Phong: 31
- Da Nang: 51

It is often easier to get a quick, clear connection calling out of Vietnam than to call another locale within Vietnam! Additionally, most offices, even large ones, do not yet have rotary phone systems. Thus, you may have to try several separate numbers listed for a particular organization to find one that is not busy. Patience is the rule!

Time

The entire country of Vietnam is located in the GMT +7 time zone, the same as Bangkok, Thailand. It is one hour earlier in Vietnam than in Hong Kong, Taipei, and Singapore and two hours earlier than in Japan. When the United States is on standard time, Vietnam is 15 hours ahead of Los Angeles and 12 hours ahead of New York. There is no daylight savings time in Vietnam.

Electricity

The electricity supply is 110 and 220 volts (50 cycles), AC. Bring a multiplug adaptor.

Business Hours

Government offices and most businesses are open six days a week, Monday through Saturday, from 7:30 or 8:00

A.M. to 11:30 A.M. and from 1:00 to 4:30 P.M. Banks are open from 8:00 A.M. to 3:00 P.M. and are closed Saturday afternoons and Sundays. Retail shops stay open late in the evening, in some cases all night. Most indoor restaurants and bars close between 11:00 P.M. and midnight, but sidewalk restaurants and cafes stay open later.

For the businessperson who will be staying a short time in Vietnam, don't overlook the fact that meetings can be book on Saturdays with both government and nongovernment offices.

National Holidays

January 1	New Year's Day
January–February	Tet (three-day Vietnamese lunar new year)
April 30	Liberation Day
May 1	Labor Day
May 19	Ho Chi Minh's birthday
September 2	National Day

In addition, Easter, Buddha's birthday, the Chinese mid-autumn festival, and Christmas are celebrated by many Vietnamese.

Water

Don't drink tap water. Avoid ice as well and watch carefully as the waiter comes around to drop big chunks of it into everyone's beer, as Vietnamese usually drink beer "on the rocks!" Ask for prechilled drinks in cans and bottles. If the particular cafe you are patronizing doesn't have these, ask them for a bucket of ice to chill your favorite beverage. Bottled mineral water is available everywhere, and you can buy a supply for your hotel refrigerator. When you buy such water from street vendors, be sure to check the seals for tampering.

Health

No vaccinations are presently required, but World Health Organization doctors recommend shots against tetanus, diphtheria, meningitis, and hepatitis as well as a polio booster. Most Western over-the-counter medicines are available in the big cities, as are antibiotics and penicillin. Of course, you should bring an extra pair of glasses or contact lenses as well as an extra supply of prescription medicines.

Business Entertainment

Saigon is exploding with restaurants and bars, karaoke lounges, and nightclubs. Here are some examples of places to socialize with or meet other businesspeople:

> Rooftop of the Rex Hotel
> 141 Nguyen Hue, District 1
> Tel: 84-8-296-046
>> This is one of the breeziest and most pleasant spots in Saigon, catering to mostly Western businesspeople. Both drinks and good Vietnamese food are served.
>
> City Bar and Grill
> 63 Dong Khoi Street, District 1
> Tel: 84-8-298-006
>> This bistro features soft live music and a California cuisine and ambiance.
>
> Tiger Tavern
> 221 Dong Khoi Street, District 1
> Tel: 84-8-222-738

This wood-paneled pub serves the coldest beer in Vietnam.

Thanh Nien Restaurant
11 Nguyen Van Chiem, District 1

This outdoor restaurant serves excellent Vietnamese food and caters to a mix of Asian and Western guests.

Vietnam House
93–95 Dong Khoi Street, District 1
Tel: 84- 8-291- 623

This is a more upscale, sophisticated Vietnamese restaurant. The bar is a popular after-work gathering place for expatriates.

Phu Son Cappuccino Restaurant
9–11 Ho Huan Nghiep, District 1
Tel: 84- 8-291- 051

This bistro serves pizza, Italian dishes, and Vietnamese food. You can sit at sidewalk tables as well if you don't mind being bothered by shoeshine boys and vendors.

Maxim's
13–17 Dong Khoi Street, District 1
Tel: 84- 8-296 - 676

This was an institution in Vietnam before 1975 and still is. It has an extensive menu and an elaborate floor show.

Givral Cafe
169 Dong Khoi Street, District 1

Broddard Cafe
131 Dong Khoi Street, District 1

There is nothing distinguished about the food at these two air-conditioned dining rooms, centrally located on Dong Khoi Street, but they are very popular places to relax, cool off, drink, and watch the world go by on the other side of the picture windows. They are also excellent places to meet other foreigners and compare travel and business notes.

Apocalypse Now
29 Mac Thi Buoi, District 1

A number of bars catering to foreigners have opened (and closed) in Saigon. The most famous is this one named after the movie. There is a pool table, a friendly English-speaking staff, a sometimes rowdy crowd of foreigners, and the sounds of the Doors, Credence Clearwater Revival, Jimi Hendrix, and the like blaring through the sound system. A poster from the movie, autographed by Martin Sheen, is proudly displayed. It's no place for a serious conversation, but it is fun for homesick American business travelers and expatriates.

In Hanoi the choices for restaurants and bars (like hotel accommodations) are limited. The bar at the Metropole (15 Ngo Quyen Street) is a key gathering spot for foreigners after work. The restaurants here and at the Saigon Hotel (80 Ly Thuong Kiet Street) serve good food.

Another popular place for expatriates and business travelers is the Sunset Pub on the top of the Dong Do Hotel on Giang Vo Street (tel: 84-4-351-382). The pub serves drinks and outstanding pizzas and hamburgers either inside or outside on the patio. Friendly, talkative customers come from all over the world, making the pub an excellent place to share experiences.

Two other choices that have been recommended are A Little Italian at 81 Tho Nhuom Street (tel: 84-4-258-167) and Piano Restaurant and Bar at 50 Hang Vai Street (tel: 84-4-232-423).

10

TWELVE INTERESTING THINGS TO DO IN YOUR FREE TIME

If you are visiting Vietnam for business, you should not pass up the opportunity to experience some of the most interesting and enjoyable activities that are now attracting a surge of tourists from all over the world. By gaining more understanding of the people and the culture, you will be in a better position to assess the marketplace.

One question I was frequently asked following my early trips to postwar Vietnam is, "How do the Vietnamese treat Americans?" Some even wondered whether I was insulted or spat on.

Nothing of the kind ever happened to me or any visitor I have met. It must be remembered that half the country—the half you are most likely to visit and do business in—was our friend and ally for many years. From the beginning, my visits to the south were greeted with effusive friendliness by businesspeople, government officials, and everyday Vietnamese. When learning that I live in California, local

Vietnamese tell me proudly of the relatives they have living in Orange County or the San Jose area. One family I met even has a son nicknamed Cali in honor of the place where much of his family has resettled.

The response of northerners is more reserved, though this is more likely a function of the cultural differences between north and south, as well as decades of isolation from westerners, than it is any rancor from the war. I have on occasion been lectured in ministerial meetings in Hanoi during the height of the dispute over the U.S. embargo—but always with a smile.

On one occasion, I was touring a former battle site and learned only afterward that the woman who guided me in a polite, friendly manner had lost three brothers (Viet Cong) in battles with Americans during the war. I never would have guessed that by the way she treated me.

The bottom line is that you can expect courtesy, friendliness, and curiosity about your own life-style. But, as was discussed in an earlier chapter, be judicious in your initiation of conversations about the war. Technical questions about what happened where and when are fine, but be cautious about asking for or giving opinions. Remember that the war represented a range of different experiences for the Vietnamese, just as it did for Americans. The person you might be talking to could be the privileged offspring of a hard-line communist family from the north, one whose relatives were wiped out by either the communist side or the American side, an individual who once worked for Americans but was left behind and feels betrayed, or one who spent years in prison after the war and is decidedly though secretly anticommunist.

Experience and enjoy the everyday people of Vietnam as well as the lively urban street scenes and beautiful varied scenery, from mountains to beaches to great pine forests to rice paddies in the countryside. For detailed tour and travel arrangements, you can make arrangements through your hotel or contact Saigontourist at 49 Le Thanh Ton Street in Ho Chi Minh City (tel: 84-8-230-102; fax: 84-8-224-987).

Here are my twelve favorite things to do in Vietnam when I have some extra time.

1. *Cyclo tour in central Saigon.* Hire a cyclo (for about $3 to $5 per hour) and spend an hour or two cruising around District 1 of Saigon, where most of the landmarks, tourist spots, ministries, companies, and shopping areas are located. The drivers hanging around your hotel usually speak some English, so you can ask questions as you ride past locations like the Notre Dame cathedral, city hall, the central post office, the zoo, the waterfront, the central market, and Dong Khoi Street, on which the most popular night spots and shops are located. Any time you want to stop, just let the driver know. This is also a great way to observe an emerging market in action: the stores, showrooms, billboards, foreign company headquarters, and new hotel and office construction.

2. *Reunification Hall (presidential palace).* In the city's center (entrance at 106 Nguyen Du Street), the former presidential offices of South Vietnamese President Nguyen Van Thieu have been preserved as they were when communist tanks crashed through the gates on April 30, 1975. A guided tour through rooms showcasing Vietnamese fine arts as well as more functionary war rooms and underground bunkers is only slightly propagandistic and is worth an hour's time between business appointments. You can sit in President Thieu's chair and imagine what it must have been like as your country crumbled around you. Reunification Hall is open daily, except Sunday, from 8:00 to 10:00 A.M. and 1:00 to 4:00 P.M.

3. *Former U.S. Embassy.* Unless you have a meeting with this building's new tenant, Petro Vietnam, all you can do is gaze at it from the sidewalk. But there it is, the site of one of the most famous images of the war, the rooftop landing pad where the last helicopter carrying U.S. personnel fled on April 29, 1975. There is intense speculation that the structure will serve an official U.S. function once again, this time as a consulate (not an embassy), as the capital of the reunified Vietnam is, of course, Hanoi. The former U.S. embassy is located on the corner of Le Duan Boulevard and Mac Dinh Street in the city's center.

4. *Cu Chi tunnels.* About an hour's drive out of Saigon, you can visit and actually crawl through part of the network of earthen tunnels and bunkers that the Viet Cong constructed to hide from U.S. forces after making their sneak attacks. And, for those who haven't had enough of guns back home, there is a firing range as well. I guess the idea is to pretend you are in (or back in) some rootin' tootin' jungle warfare. What fun! Saigontourist, your hotel, or your driver can bring you out and back in half a day.

5. *Saigon River cruise.* Ask your cyclo driver to pedal you to the waterfront and help you arrange a small motorized launch to cruise up and down the Saigon River. Be sure to negotiate the exact price and duration of the journey in advance (typical price is $10 per hour). Bring cold drinks, snacks, a camera, and perhaps a business contact or two and get a good feel for this port city and life along the river as you socialize.

6. *Mekong Delta.* Southerners consider the Mekong delta the true heart of the country. You can

arrange a personal trip or an organized day tour to take you by car and ferry to the delta cities of My Tho and Can Tho and learn more about how most Vietnamese live.

7. *Vung Tau.* This is the most popular beach resort in the south, more because of its proximity to Saigon than the quality of the beach and facilities. But a day trip organized privately or through Saigontourist gives you a chance to see seacoast life in Vietnam as well as the onshore center and processing zone for offshore oil activities. The bumpy two-hour ride each way will also demonstrate to you, the "hard" way, why improving the infrastructure is such a priority for the Vietnamese!

8. *Da Nang–Hue trip.* If you are in Da Nang and have a full day, hire a car and driver at your hotel (for about $50) and drive along the mountainous coastal highway to the ancient capital of Hue. Your driver will take you to the most important historical sights. Have lunch on a floating restaurant on the Perfume River, do a little more sightseeing, and then return. The drive itself is worth the price of admission, for the mountain and coastal scenery rivals the views on California's Pacific Coast Highway.

9. *Cyclo tour in central Hanoi.* Like you did in Saigon, hire a cyclo to take you around this beautiful, interesting city, particularly the Hoan Kiem Lake area (where most international companies moving into Hanoi are locating) and the nearby old French quarter.

10. *Ho Chi Minh mausoleum and birthplace, Hanoi.* No matter how you feel about "Uncle Ho," it is fascinating to see the trappings of reverence and ritual that the Vietnamese have orchestrated for their leader. President Ho's embalmed remains

are housed inside a glass case inside a huge concrete tomb. Visitors line up in groups and are escorted by uniformed guards for a quick look. No cameras, talking, sunglasses, or hands in pockets allowed! Nearby, in a pleasant setting, you can visit Ho's modest house, study, and wartime conference room as well as the One-Pillar Pagoda, one of the most frequently photographed landmarks in Vietnam. The mausoleum is open mornings, except for Mondays and Fridays.

11. *Ha Long Bay.* If you have two days and have already had a chance to explore Hanoi, I strongly recommend you hire a car and driver (for about $80) and visit Ha Long Bay, a four- to five-hour drive northeast of Hanoi on the coast. The trip is an education on many levels. During the first part of the journey, you experience the deplorable condition of the road linking Vietnam's second and third largest cities, Hanoi and Hai Phong. Two river crossings are accomplished by ferry as there are no bridges. Once in Ha Long, your driver will find you a hotel, most likely a dilapidated but beautiful French-style villa overlooking the bay. In the afternoon, rent your own private boat for $5 to $10 per hour, bring snacks and drinks, and cruise around the hundreds of limestone islands that jut out of the sea. Your captain will anchor so you can explore some of the caves on the larger formations. And, any time you want, he will anchor so that you can dive off the side of your boat for a cool swim. Head back to Hanoi right after breakfast the next morning.

12. *Veterans' tours.* Saigontourist offers special tours for veterans who wish to visit places such as the DMZ, Dong Ha, Quang Tri, Khe Sanh, Hamburger Hill, and the Ho Chi Minh Trail. Here is

how the tours are explained in Saigontourist's promotional literature:

> War veteran tours have been set up by Vietnamese veterans for their foreign counterparts of the two Indochina wars. These are special tour programs for those who have served in Vietnam and now wish to revisit former locations and areas of their former units, of the Viet Cong war zones and especially former battlefields.
> The motto of Saigontourist is to promote understanding and friendship, thus helping to heal war wounds.

For details and booking, contact Saigontourist.

For additional, detailed tourist information, there are several useful travel guides now on the market. The most popular is Lonely Planet's *Vietnam: A Travel Survival Kit*, published in several languages.

11

Sample Itinerary for Your Exploratory Mission

Here is a model itinerary for an "on-your-own" introductory trip to Vietnam. It has been designed for those who can afford just one week away. Ideally, you should spend more time in Vietnam, so expand this schedule if at all possible. If you do have more time, consider doing the following:

- Visit the areas surrounding Ho Chi Minh City, including the Mekong delta cities of Can Tho and My Tho, and the coastal city of Vung Tau, a major tourist site as well as the onshore center for offshore oil activities.
- Spend more time in both Ho Chi Minh City and Hanoi following up on your initial contacts, particularly those who could be potential customers or business partners.
- Visit cultural and historical sights such as the Cu Chi tunnels, Ha Long Bay, and the Ho Chi Minh mausoleum and surrounding area. (For my personal favorites, see chapter 10.)

- Include a visit to the Da Nang-Hue area as you make your way from Ho Chi Minh City to Hanoi. Business opportunities here are sometimes overlooked, and the historical sights and natural beauty are spectacular. You can fly via Vietnam Airlines from Ho Chi Minh City to Da Nang in one hour; after your stopover, continue on another flight directly to Hanoi.

Costs cited are to be taken as estimates only. The trips are planned for those with moderate budgets. In other words, I have assumed that you neither want to rough it nor live high on the hog. Contact numbers for many of the organizations listed in the schedules can be found in chapters 9, 12, and 13.

INTRODUCTORY TRIP TO VIETNAM

Saturday

- Flight from the United States to Hong Kong
- Airlines with nonstop service from the West Coast: Delta, United, Cathay Pacific, and Singapore
- Approximate cost
    - Roundtrip coach from West Coast: $1,200
    - Roundtrip business class from West Coast: $2,200
    - Or, use those frequent-flier miles for this portion of the trip!

Sunday

- Arrive in Hong Kong in the evening and transfer to a hotel
- Hotel cost: $150 and up

Monday

- During the day
  - Meet with the Vietnam Business Association, the American Chamber of Commerce, and one or more of their members doing business in Vietnam who are in fields related to yours
- Evening
  - Hong Kong–Ho Chi Minh City, Cathay Pacific Flight 765, 7:00–8:30 P.M. (one-hour time change)
  - Transfer to the Rex or a similar hotel
  - Approximate costs: roundtrip flight in and out of Vietnam: $550; hotel: $80 per night

Tuesday

- Morning
  - Place calls to confirm and set up appointments
  - Walk to Vietnam Airlines and/or Saigontourist to make travel arrangements to Hanoi
- Throughout the day
  - Introductory meetings with the Vietnam Chamber of Commerce and Industry, the Ho Chi Minh City People's Committee, the State Committee for Cooperation and Investment, and the Foreign Investment Service Company; schedule meetings specific to your business activity for the next day on the basis of suggestions made at these meetings
- Evening
  - Have drinks or dinner with an American consultant, lawyer, or businessperson operating in Vietnam

Wednesday

- Early morning
  - Cyclo tour around major markets and sights in central Saigon
- Throughout the day and evening
  - Continue appointment, focusing on specific ministry and companies relevant to your industry

Thursday

- Morning
  - Ho Chi Minh City–Hanoi, Vietnam Airlines Flight 214, 8:30–10:30 A.M. (no time change)
  - Transfer to the Saigon or a similar hotel
  - Approximate cost: flight: $150; hotel: $100 per night
- Afternoon
  - Meetings with the Hanoi People's Committee, the Vietnam Chamber of Commerce and Industry, the Ministry of Trade and Tourism, the State Committee for Cooperation and Investment, and other ministries and Vietnamese companies relevant to your business activity
- Evening
  - Have drinks or dinner at Metropole with American or other foreign businesspeople based in Hanoi

Friday

- Morning
  - Cyclo tour to the major markets and sights of Hanoi

- Throughout the day
    - Continue program of meetings and visits to facilities
- Evening
    - Have drinks and dinner at the Sunset Pub with foreign businesspeople

Saturday

- Morning
    - Hanoi–Hong Kong, Cathay Pacific Flight 790, 10:05 A.M.–12:50 P.M. (one-hour time change)
    - Transfer to hotel

Sunday

- Return flight to the United States, arriving the same day

12

DIRECTORY OF ORGANIZATIONS THAT CAN HELP YOU

The following list of organizations, support groups, and service companies can help you do business in Vietnam—from your initial forays into the market to the licensing process to on-the-ground operations once you are there.

This list is not exhaustive. There is a growing legion of consultants as well as public relations, marketing, accounting, law, and advertising firms serving the Vietnamese market.

Should you decide to go the consultant route, check references thoroughly, particularly prior and current clients. If you plan to rely on a larger, more established law or accounting firm or investment services company, be sure that adequate attention is given to your account and that their more expensive services fit into your budget.

Presence on this list does not constitute an endorsement, only that my own experience and research has determined that they are active players in this relatively new

173

field. (Neither the author nor the publisher has any financial link of any kind, implied or explicit, with any of the mentioned organizations.)

Some of these organizations require membership, charge fees for services, or both. Yet, although competition to provide services to would-be investors and traders is growing, a friendly camaraderie remains among those who have staked out a pioneering role in Vietnam. Most will be willing to talk to you at the outset without charge and will point you in the right direction (hopefully *their* direction!) as you take your initial steps.

IN THE UNITED STATES

The U.S.-Vietnam Trade Council
731 8th Street S.E.
Washington, D.C. 20003
Tel: 202-547-3800
Contact: Virginia Foote, executive director

The Vietnam-America Chamber of Commerce
31 West 52nd Street
New York, N.Y. 10019
Tel: 212-841-0781
Contact: Irwin Jay Robinson, president

East-West Center
1777 East-West Road
Honolulu, Hawaii 96848
Tel: 808-944-7111
Fax: 808-944-7376

America Vietnam Trade Development Council
1919 Pennsylvania Avenue N.W., Suite 30
Washington, D.C. 20006
Tel: 202-736-2184
Fax: 202-223-6739

U.S. Department of Commerce
14th Street and Constitution Avenue N.W.
Washington, D.C. 20230
Tel: 202-482-2000
- International Trade Administration
  Tel: 202-482-3917
- Bureau of Trade Development
  Tel: 202-482-1461
- U.S. Foreign and Commercial Service
  Tel: 202-482-5777

Office of U.S. Trade Representative
600 17th Street N.W.
Washington, D.C. 20506
Tel: 202-395-3230

California Chamber of Commerce
1201 K Street
Sacramento, Calif. 95814
Tel: 916-444-6670
Fax: 916-444-6685
Contact: Susanne Stirling, international vice president

This chamber keeps abreast of experts in the field, delegations going to or coming from Vietnam, and policy development.

California Southeast Asia Business Council
1946 Embarcadero, Suite 200
Oakland, Calif. 94606
Tel: 510-536-1967
Fax: 510-261-9598
Contact: Ms. Jeremy Potash, executive director

This group has conducted a business mission to Vietnam and holds frequent seminars and meetings featuring experts on Vietnam and top government officials.

Vietnamese Chamber of Commerce in Orange County
9938 Bolsa Avenue, Suite 216
Westminster, Calif. 92683
Tel: 714-839-2257
Fax: 714-775-7270
Contact: Dr. Co Pham, president
> This chamber is good for making contact with that segment of the overseas Vietnamese business community that welcomes commercial relations between the United States and Vietnam.

Skadden, Arps, Slate, Meagher & Flom
919 Third Avenue
New York, N.Y. 10022
Tel: 212-735-3000
Fax: 212-735-2000
Contact: Thomas J. Schwarz, partner
> This law firm and its key attorney, Thomas J. Schwarz, offer legal and other services related to setting up and conducting business operations in Vietnam.

Vietnam Investment Information and Consulting (VIIC)
3709 Convoy Street, Suite 206
San Diego, Calif. 92111
Tel: 619-277-5580
Fax: 619-277-9411
Contact: Mr. Giang Tran, president
> This firm organized Vietnamerica Expo '94 in Hanoi in April 1994. It is a for-profit firm providing a variety of trade and investment consulting services as well as representation for foreign companies out of its Hanoi and Ho Chi Minh City offices.

Vietnam America Trade and Investment Consulting Company (VATICO)
1150 17th Street N.W., Suite 600
Washington, D.C. 20036
Tel: 202-872-1200

This is the first U.S. consulting firm to station an American full time in a Hanoi office.

Incontra, Inc.
565 Fifth Avenue
New York, N.Y. 10017
Tel: 212-697-1558
Fax: 212-697-2609

This is the U.S. agent for the Vietnam Chamber of Commerce and Industry's Trade Service Company (for details, see the entry below for the Chamber of Commerce and Industry of Vietnam).

A-Plus Travel
767 North Hill Street, Suite 112
Los Angeles, Calif. 90012
Tel: 213-617-3581
Contact: Ms. Gina Tran

This Vietnamese-owned travel agency has a reliable track record for securing visas, hotels, and other Vietnam-related travel services.

IN HONG KONG

Hong Kong is a vital center for information and contacts related to doing business in Vietnam, one reason being that many of the regional headquarters of multinational companies are based in Hong Kong and have been assigned to the task of preparing their firms' entry to Vietnam. In addition, Hong Kong is the region's premier business and trade center.

The American Chamber of Commerce in Hong Kong
1030 Swire House
Central, Hong Kong
Tel: 852-526-0165

Fax: 852-810-1289
Contact: Frank Martin, president

This chamber and its Indochina committee have been extremely active in information gathering, trade missions, and policy work related to Vietnam. At modest cost, the chamber, through its Business Briefing Program, will assemble a team of businesspeople and others to brief you on specific opportunities in Vietnam relevant to your business.

Vietnam Business Association of Hong Kong
912 One Pacific Place
88 Queensway
Central, Hong Kong
Tel: 852-530-3267
Fax: 852-530-3452
Contact: Penelope N. Post, executive director

This group has as its members many of the early pioneers in the postwar Vietnamese market: lawyers, Hong Kong executives, regional managers of international companies, bankers, and consultants. A good group for making contacts, the VBA frequently hosts forums, seminars, and visits by Vietnamese officials.

Hong Kong Trade Development Council
38th Floor, Office Tower, Convention Plaza
1 Harbour Road
Wanchai, Hong Kong
Tel: 852-584-4333
Fax: 852-824-0249
Contact: Research Department

The HKTDC's purpose is to facilitate trade with all countries, and it maintains an extensive trade reference library and a trade leads system with valuable information on the Vietnamese market. The library is open free of charge during normal business hours and also publishes and sells informative newsletters and market studies.

Infocus
Wilson House, Suite 1004
19–27 Wyndham Street
Central, Hong Kong
Tel: 852-868-0722
Fax: 852-523-5196
Contact: Shawna Stonehouse, managing director
> Through a formal agreement with Vietnamese officials, Infocus conducts seminars, business missions, and matchmaking in Vietnam, Hong Kong, and other locations.

Skadden, Arps, Slate, Meagher & Flom
30/F Peregrine Tower, Lippo Centre
89 Queensway
Central, Hong Kong
Tel: 852-820-0700
Fax: 852-820-0727
    852-820-0728
Contact: Raymond W. Vickers, partner
> This law firm and its key attorney, Raymond W. Vickers, offer legal and other services.

Ernst & Young
Hutchison House, 15th Floor
10 Harcourt Road
Central, Hong Kong
Tel: 852-846-9888
Fax: 852-868-4432
Contact: John Harvey, director
> This "Big Six" CPA firm is now fully licensed for operations in Vietnam and has more than sixty staff working in its Hanoi and Ho Chi Minh City offices.

Deloitte Touche Tohmatsu International
Suite 1908, Wing On Centre
111 Connaught Road
Central, Hong Kong
Tel: 852-545-5811

Fax: 852-854-0076
Contacts: David Tong, Christine Tran

Bank of America
20th Floor, Bank of America Tower
12 Harcourt Road
Central, Hong Kong
Tel: 852-847-6965
Fax: 852-847-6494
Contact: Luu H. Le, Indochina representative

   This bank has recently opened a Hanoi office as well.

Vietnamese Visa Office
Kam Chung Building, 20th Floor
19 Hennessy Road
Central, Hong Kong
Tel: 852-529-1787

   This office was set up by the Vietnamese government to handle the growing number of visa applications in Hong Kong.

In Thailand

Citibank
127 Sathorn Road
Bangkok, 10120
Tel: 66-2-21320007
Fax: 66-2-2132527
Contact: Robert A. Wilson, Jr., regional manager

In Vietnam

Chamber of Commerce and Industry of Vietnam (VCCI)
Hanoi: 33 Ba Trieu Street
           Tel: 84-42-56446

Fax: 84-42-53023
Contact: International Relations Department

Ho Chi Minh City: 171 Vo Thi Sau Street, District 3
Tel: 84-8-230-301
Fax: 84-8-294-472

This national chamber (sometimes referred to as the VIETCO Chamber or VCCI), initiated by the government but now a nongovernmental agency, is the key link between the Vietnamese business community, the international business community, and the government. The chamber's mission is to promote and assist trade, investment, and other business activities in Vietnam and abroad. Functions and services include the following:

- Conducts dialogue with the government to influence policies affecting business
- Assists overseas businesspeople and delegations with services including visas, business appointments, identifying potential partners, and travel arrangements
- Provides a calendar of trade fairs and exhibitions
- Supplies trade information, including publications like the *Vietnam Business Directory,* which lists thousands of local companies and their commercial activities, and *Vietnam Foreign Trade,* a quarterly magazine
- Issues certificates of origin and other documents used in international trade
- Registers patents and trademarks
- Provides consultancy services

Many of these services are provided through the VCCI's Trade Services Company. The chamber also maintains the Vietnam International Arbitration Center, which is designed to resolve disputes with foreign-invested companies.

Foreign Investment Service Company (FISC)
12 Nam Ky Khoi Nghia, District 1
Ho Chi Minh City, Vietnam
Tel: 84-8-291-100
Fax: 84-8-298-434
Contact: Dr. Pham Khac Chi, general director

Hanoi: 108 Le Duan Street
            Tel: 84- 4-515-267
            Fax: 84- 4-260-724

The FISC is a full-service investment services company affiliated with the Ministry of Trade that will help you with every aspect of your foray into the Vietnamese market, including introducing you to senior ministry officials and businesspeople, helping you steer your business application through the bureaucracy, and counseling you on business options. The FISC was the first Vietnamese entity I worked with, and the services provided to me have always been professional and worthwhile.

Saigontourist
49 Le Thanh Ton Street, District 1
Ho Chi Minh City
Tel: 84- 8-230-102
Fax: 84- 8-224-987

Saigontourist owns many major hotels and restaurants and books travel arrangements and programs for individual travelers and groups.

INVESTIP
39 Tran Hung Dao
Hanoi
Tel: 84-42-264-707
Fax: 84-42-398-540

Skadden, Arps, Slate, Meagher & Flom
29 Han Thuyen Street

Hanoi
Tel: 84-4-261-236
Fax: 84-4-261-237
Contact: Eugene A. Matthews

Law Firm of Russin & Vecchi
8 Nguyen Hue, 6th Floor
Ho Chi Minh City
Tel: 84- 8-243-026
Fax: 84- 8-243-113
Contact: Michael Scown, attorney at law

Price Waterhouse
The Hanoi Business Center
51 Ly Thai To Street, Hanoi
Tel: 84- 4-266 -122
Fax: 84- 4-266031

Kingship Limited Vietnam Consultants
8 Trang Thi, Hanoi
Tel: 84- 4-260043
Fax: 84- 4-260262
Contact: Mathilde Genovese

Business Centers

Ho Chi Minh City: 49–57 Dong Du Street, District 1
　　　　　　　　　Tel: 84- 8-297-777
　　　　　　　　　Fax: 84- 8-298-155

Hanoi:　51 Ly Thai To Street
　　　　Tel: 84- 42-66122
　　　　Fax: 84- 42-66030

Da Nang:　Vietnam Chamber of Commerce and Industry
　　　　　172 Bach Dang
　　　　　Tel: 84-51-22930

Selected Trading Companies in Vietnam

The Hong Kong Trade Development Council has culled this representative sampling of licensed trading companies from various sources. For further listings in your field, contact the Ministry of Trade and Tourism, the Vietnam Chamber of Commerce and Industry, the Hong Kong Trade Development Council, and the Hanoi and Ho Chi Minh City telephone directories and Yellow Pages.

Vietnam National Vegetables and Fruit Corporation
Trung Tu, Dong Da District
Hanoi
Tel: 84-4-263-396
Fax: 84-4-263-926

   Export: fruits
   Import: equipment and materials for fruit and vegetable processing

Vietnam National Coffee Export-Import Corporation
5 Ong Ich Khiem Street
Hanoi
Tel: 84-4-262-382
Fax: 84-4-256422

   Export: coffee beans, instant coffee
   Import: machinery, equipment, chemicals

Vietnam National Foodstuffs Import-Export Corporation
58 Ly Thai To Street
Hanoi
Tel: 84-4-255-768
Fax: 84-4-255-476

   Export: confectioneries, drinks
   Import: equipment, materials, chemicals for breweries and food processing

Vietnam National Metals Corporation
D2, Khuong Thuong Area

Hanoi
Tel: 84-4-262657

> Export: semifinished and finished metal products, scrap metal
> Import: various kinds of metal

Vietnam National Sea Products Export-Import Corporation
87 Ham Nghi Street, District 1
Ho Chi Minh City
Tel: 84-8-291-333
Fax: 84-8-290-146

> Export: frozen and dried sea products
> Import: equipment and spare parts for food processing

Central Food Corporation II
42 Chu Manh Trinh, District 1
Ho Chi Minh City
Tel: 84-8-230-243
Fax: 84-8-292-344

> Export: rice, flour
> Import: material and equipment for agriculture

Vietnam Garment Manufacture, Import-Export Corporation
32 Trang Tien Street
Hanoi
Tel: 84-4-253-604

> Export: garments
> Import: equipment and spare parts for garment industry

Union of Textile Production and Import Export Corporation
2 Mai Dong Street
Hanoi
Tel: 84-4-257-700
Fax: 84-4-263-611

Export: textile yarns, knitwear, ready-made clothes
Import: raw cotton, synthetic fibers, machinery and spare parts

Union of Leather and Footwear Manufacturing and Export-Import Enterprises
14 Nguyen Hue Street, District 1
Ho Chi Minh City
Tel: 84-8-291-209
Fax: 84-8-299-217

Export: preserved and tanned hides and skins
Import: machinery and equipment

Vietnam National General Export-Import Corporation I
46 Ngo Quyen Street
Hanoi
Tel: 84-4-257-555
Fax: 84-4-259-894

Major activities: general traders on behalf of production and trading organizations

Vietnam National General Export-Import Corporation II
66 Pho Duc Chinh Street, District 1
Ho Chi Minh City
Tel: 84-8-293-935
Fax: 84-8-292-968

Major activities: general traders on behalf of production and trading organizations

Vietnam National Oil Equipment and Technology Import Corporation
194 Nam Ky Khoi Nghia Street
Ho Chi Minh City
Tel: 84-8-293-633
Fax: 84-8-299-686

Export: crude oil
Import: equipment and technology for oil exploration

FINAL NOTE: U.S. GOVERNMENT ASSISTANCE IN VIETNAM

At the time of publication, the Vietnamese and American governments had just agreed to establish liaison offices in their respective capitals that would serve many of the functions of embassies until full diplomatic relations were established.

The agreement includes the posting of approximately ten U.S. diplomats in Hanoi and ten Vietnamese diplomats in Washington, D.C. A search for a suitable location is under way. Once these embassies open, American business travelers can expect to rely on them for basic services, information, and emergencies.

However, when it comes to providing services to facilitate the expansion of commercial relations, Washington is still moving slowly. Thus, the U.S. government cannot be counted on at this time for significant support.

The California–Southeast Asia Business Council recently delineated current policy in a recent communication with its members:

> If you thought the lifting of the embargo in February, 1994 meant that U.S. government agencies would at last be in a position to help American firms make up for lost time, not so fast. Not only is there no commercial representation in place, but Eximbank, Overseas Private Investment Corp., Trade Development Agency, USAID and other agencies are still barred from providing support.
>
> Fortunately, the National Security Council has just loosened things up. NSC has cleared the way for working-level USDOC and USDA personnel (up to deputy assistant secretary-level) to contact and meet with Vietnamese officials at exhibitions and trade shows in third countries, and to contact such officials for information about doing business in Vietnam. Also, senior-level U.S. officials may now write to Vietnamese officials to

support the efforts of individual U.S. companies to gain contract awards in Vietnam.

Specifically disapproved by NSC were proposed Ag trade missions and promotional events in Vietnam, establishment of two Foreign Commercial Service posts for the pending liaison office in Hanoi, and some proposed commercial-related travel by senior-level U.S. officials.

13

Directory of Government Offices and Current Officials

Because of the role they play in the economy, Vietnamese government officials and ministries will form a key part of your network for doing business. The most important names and numbers are listed below.

Please note when calling or faxing from outside of Vietnam that you must begin with the country code (84), followed by the appropriate city or provincial code (e.g., 8 for Ho Chi Minh City, 4 for Hanoi) and then the local number.

You should also be aware that many individuals answering the phone speak little or no English. If a fax number is available, that is the better way to make your initial contact. Another option is to have a Vietnamese-speaking person make the first call for you.

Finally, although promptly responding to a fax may seem like a simple business courtesy to most of us, in Vietnam it is an expensive proposition. Even when you make a specific request or proposal, unless you are dealing with a major organization, you may not get a response. A good approach is to use the fax to introduce yourself and your interests, inform the receiver of the dates you will be in Vietnam, and promise to call as soon as you are in Vietnam to lock in a meeting.

SENIOR NATIONAL-LEVEL OFFICIALS

Secretary of the Communist Party of Vietnam:
Mr. Do Muoi

President of the Socialist Republic of Vietnam:
Mr. Le Duc Anh

Prime Minister: Mr. Vo Van Kiet

    Office of Government
    Address: Bach Thao, Hanoi
    Tel: 258-241

    Foreign Economic Relations Department
    Director: Mr. Le Manh Tuan
    Tel: 254-964

Chairman of the National Assembly:
Mr. Nong Duc Manh

    Office of the National Assembly
    Address: 35 Ngo Quyen, Hanoi
    Tel: 252-861
    Director: Mr. Vu Mao

    Department for External Relations
    Director: Mr. Tran Xuan Anh
    Tel: 252-861, ext. 3115

MINISTRIES AND MINISTERIAL-LEVEL AGENCIES

State Committee for Cooperation and Investment (SCCI)
  Address: 56 Quoc Tu Giam, Hanoi
  Tel: 253-666, 254-970
  Fax: 259-271
  Chairman: Mr. Dau Ngoc Xuan
  First vice chairman: Dr. Nguyen Mai
  Ho Chi Minh City Office
  Address: 178 Nguyen Dinh Chieu, District 3
  Tel: 94674, 91534
  Fax: 291-534
  Vice chairman: Mr. Nguyen Van Ich

State Bank of Vietnam
  Address: 49 Ly Thai To, Hanoi
  Tel: 252-831
  Fax: 258-385
  Governor: Mr. Cao Si Kiem
  Department of External Relations
  Director: Mr. Nguyen Cong Hai
  Tel: 265-589

Ministry of Agriculture and Food Industry
  Address: Bach Thao, Hanoi
  Tel: 268-161
  Minister: Mr. Nguyen Cong Tan
  International Cooperation Department
  Director: Mr. Nguyen Van Phuoc
  Tel: 259-672
  Fax: 254-319

Ministry of Construction
  Address: 37 Le Dai Hahn, Hanoi
  Tel: 254-171
  Minister: Mr. Ngo Xuan Loc

International Relations Department
Director: Mr. Le Doan Phach
Tel: 255-497
Fax: 252-153

Ministry of Culture and Information
Address: 51–53 Ngo Quyen, Hanoi
Tel: 262-975
Fax: 267-101
Minister: Mr. Tran Hoan

International Relations Department
Director: Mr. Vuong Thinh
Tel: 264-287

Ministry of Education and Training
Address: 49 Dai Co Viet, Hanoi
Tel: 262-250
Fax: 263-243
Minister: Mr. Tran Hong Quan

International Cooperation Department
Director: Mr. Tran Va Nhung
Tel: 262-395
Fax: 259-226

Ministry of Energy
Address: 18 Tran Nguyen Han, Hanoi
Tel: 253-522
Fax: 259-226
Minister: Mr. Thai Phung Ne

Department of International Cooperation
Director: Mr. Nguyen Sy Phong
Tel: 263-725

Ministry of Finance
Address: 8 Phan Huy Chu, Hanoi
Tel: 253-869
Minister: Mr. Ho Tel

International Relations Department
Director: Mr. Nguyen Ba Toan
Tel: 262-061

Ministry of Fisheries

Address: 57 Ngoc Khanh, Hanoi
Tel: 256-396
Fax: 254-702
Minister: Mr. Nguyen Tan Trinh

International Cooperation Department
Director: Mr. Ho Van Hoanh
Tel: 254-709

Ministry of Foreign Affairs

Address: 1 Ton That Dam, Hanoi
Tel: 258-201
Minister: Mr. Nguyen Manh Cam

Department of Protocol
Director: Mr. Pham Quoc Bao
Tel: 258-201, ext. 242

America Department
Director: Mr. Nguyen Xuan Phong
Tel: 257-279
Fax: 259-205

Ministry of Forestry

Address: 123 Lo Duc, Hanoi
Tel: 253-236
Fax: 254-542
Minister: Mr. Nguyen Quang Ha

International Relations Department
Director: Mr. Bui Xuan Yen
Tel: 211-159

Ministry of Health

Address: 138 Duong Giang Vo, Hanoi
Tel: 264-051
Minister: Professor Nguyen Trong Nhan

Ministry of Heavy Industry
  Address: 54 Hai Ba Trung, Hanoi
  Tel: 258-311
  Minister: Mr. Tran Lum
  International Cooperation Department
  Director: Mr. Nguyen Xuan Chuan
  Tel: 258-311, ext. 17

Ministry of the Interior
  Address: 14 Tran Binh Trong, Hanoi
  Tel: 258-300
  Minister: Mr. Bui Thien Ngo

Ministry of Justice
  Address: 25 Cat Linh, Hanoi
  Tel: 253-395
  Fax: 254-835
  Minister: Mr. Nguyen Dinh Loc
  International Relations Department
  Acting Director: Mr. Ha Hung Cuong
  Tel: 255-316, ext. 32

Ministry of Labor, War Invalids and Social Affairs
  Address: 12 Ngo Quyen, Hanoi
  Tel: 252-236
  Minister: Mr. Tran Dinh Hoan

Ministry of Light Industry
  Address: 7 Trang Thi, Hanoi
  Tel: 255-132
  Fax: 265-303
  Minister: Mr. Dang Vu Chu
  International Relations Department
  Director: Mr. Nguyen Hieu
  Tel: 252-852

Ministry of Sciences, Technology and Environment
  Address: 39 Tran Hung Dao, Hanoi
  Tel: 252-731
  Minister: Mr. Dang Huu

Department for International Cooperation
Director: Mr. Dau Dinh Loi
Tel: 263-388

National Information and Documentation Centre for Science and Technology
Address: 24 Ly Thuong Kiet, Hanoi
Tel: 263-127
Director: Dr. Nguyen Van Khanh

National Office for Inventions
Address: 96–98 Nguyen Trai, Hanoi
Tel: 243-069
Director: Dr. Doan Phuong

Ministry of Trade
Address: 31 Trang Tien, Hanoi
Tel: 254-915
Fax: 264-696
Minister: Mr. Le Van Triet

Ministry of Transport and Communications
Address: 80 Tran Hung Dao, Hanoi
Tel: 254-042
Fax: 267-291
Minister: Professor Dr. Bui Danh Luu

International Relations Department
Director: Mr. Pham Van Danh
Tel: 254-012

Vietnam Civil Aviation Administration
Address: Gia Lam Airport
Tel: 272-241
Fax: 272-240
Director general: Mr. Nguyen Hong Nhi

Vietnam Railways
Address: 118 Le Duan, Hanoi
Tel: 254-998
Director general: Mr. Doan Van Xe

Vietnam Road Administration
Address: 80 Tran Hung Dao, Hanoi
Tel: 251-118
Fax: 267-291
Director general: Mr. Nguyen Dinh Tuat

Vietnam Inland Waterways Administration
Address: 80 Tran Hung Dao, Hanoi
Tel: 261-889
Fax: 250-788
Director general: Dr. Ngo Xuan Son

Vietnam National Maritime Bureau
Address: 11 Vo Thi Sau, Hai Phong
Tel: 31-46368
Fax: 31-45119
Chairman: Professor Dr. Dinh Ngoc Vien

Ministry of Water Resources
Address: 21 Lo Su, Hanoi
Tel: 258-141
Fax: 256-929
Minister: Mr. Nguyen Canh Dinh

Major People's Committees

People's Committee of Hanoi
Address: 79 Dinh Tien Hoang, Hanoi
Tel: 253-870
Chairman: Mr. Le At Hoi

External Economic Relations Bureau
Address: 81 Dinh Tien Hoang, Hanoi
Tel: 253-870
Director: Prof. Dr. Le Van Vien

People's Committee of Ho Chi Minh City
   Address: 86 Le Thanh Ton, District 1, HCMC
   Tel: 91054
   Chairman: Mr. Truong Tan Sang
   External Relations Services
   Director: Mr. Vu Hac Bong

People's Committee of Da Nang
   Address: 34 Bach Dang, Da Nang
   Tel: (51) 21286
   Chairman: Mr. Tran Dinh Dam
   Foreign Economic Relations Department
   Head: Mr. Luong Minh Sam
   Tel: (51) 21878

OTHER USEFUL NUMBERS IN HANOI

Customs Office
   Address: 51 Nguyen Van Cu
   Tel: 263-951

Entry-Exit Permit Department
   Address: 40A Hang Bai Street
   Tel: 255-798

Foreign Investment Service Company
   Address: 108 Le Duan Street
   Tel: 515-267
   Fax: 260-724

INVESTIP
   Address: 1 Bis Yet Kieu Street
   Tel: 266-185
   Fax: 266-185
   Managing Director: Mr. Le Tu

General Post Office
   Address: 18 Nguyen Du Street

Petro Vietnam
   Address: 80 Nguyen Du Street
   Tel: 257-004

Vietnam Chamber of Commerce and Industry
   Address: 33 Ba Trieu Street
   Tel: 253-023
   Fax: 256-446

Vietcombank (Foreign Trade Bank)
   Address: 7 Le Lai
   President: Mr. Nguyen Manh Thuy

Vietnam Insurance General Company
   Address: 7 Ly Thuong Kiet Street
   Tel: 262-632

Vietnam Investment Review
   Address: 35 Nha Chung Street
   Tel: 250-537
   Fax: 257-937

Vietnam National Administration of Tourism
   Address: 80 Quan Su
   Tel: 252-280
   Fax: 261-115

Vietnam Post and Telecommunications
   Address: 18 Nguyen Du
   Tel: 256-936
   Fax: 255-581
   Director general: Mr. Nguyen Ba

Vietnam Tourism
   Address: 30A Ly Thuong Kiet Street
   Tel: 264-319

Directory of Government Offices and Current Officials **199**

OTHER USEFUL NUMBERS IN HO CHI MINH CITY

City Customs Office
  Address: 21 Ton Duc Thang, District 1
  Tel: 290-912

City Post Office
  Address: 125 Ha Ba Trung, District 1
  Tel: 293-310

Export Development Center
  Address: 92–96 Nguyen Hue Boulevard, District 1
  Tel: 290-072

Foreign Investment Service Company
  Address: 12 Nam Ky Khoi Nghia Street, District 1
  Tel: 222-982
  Fax: 298-434

Saigontourist
  Address: 49 Le Thanh Ton Street, District 1
  Tel: 230-103
  Fax: 224-987

Vietnam Chamber of Commerce and Industry
  Address: 171 Vo Thi Sau, District 3
  Tel: 230-301

Vietnam Investment Review
  Address: 122 Nguyen Thi Minh Khai, District 3
  Tel: 222-423
  Fax: 231-699

Vietnam Post and Telecommunications
  Address: 137 Pasteur Street, District 3
  Tel: 294-111

14

INFORMATION RESOURCES

Comprehensive news coverage and other information about business developments in Vietnam can be hard to come by, especially if you are sitting in an office half a world away. In the United States, the *Wall Street Journal* and the *Los Angeles Times* make the most serious effort to follow commercial issues and trends. Several of the Vietnamese-language publications emanating from Orange County, California, do as well.

If your travels take you to Southeast Asia or if you have an office in the region, you should take note that English-language dailies such as Hong Kong's *South China Morning Post,* the *Bangkok Post,* the *Straights-Times* of Singapore, and the *Asian Wall Street Journal* all contain far more comprehensive coverage than is available in the United States.

For completely independent coverage of all aspects of the Vietnamese economy and society, the best resource published outside Vietnam is the *Far East Economic Review,* a weekly magazine to which you can subscribe worldwide. To subscribe, contact *Far East Economic Review,* GPO Box 160, Hong Kong (tel: 852-508-4300; fax: 852-503-1553); annual subscription: $140.

The best resource published in Vietnam is the *Vietnam Investment Review,* a weekly newspaper that chronicles and analyzes all economic and business developments in great detail. It is must reading for anyone actually doing business in Vietnam. The advertising is educational as well because it helps you assess what others are doing in the market. Ads also provide good leads on office space and expatriate housing. Although the paper understandably treads carefully when discussing noncommercial topics, business coverage appears to be generally open.

Subscriptions are offered worldwide. To inquire about subscribing or advertising, contact *Vietnam Investment Review,* 35 Nha Chung Street, Hanoi (tel: 84-4-266-740; fax: 84-4-257-937), or 122 Nguyen Thi Minh Khai, District 1, Ho Chi Minh City (tel: 84-8-222-440; fax: 84-8-231-699); annual subscription in the United States: $350.

In addition, there is the Hong Kong-based *Business News Indochina,* a monthly newsletter that emphasizes critical analysis rather than note reporting of deals and projects. The writing is lively and informative. To inquire about subscriptions, contact *Business News Indochina,* GPO Box 9794, Hong Kong (tel: 852-880-0307; fax: 852-856-1184).

When traveling in Vietnam, you will also come across several publications that, although providing the "official" view of development, keep you in the know about which companies are in Vietnam and what they are doing.

You are likely to find a small English-language daily called the *Vietnam News* in your hotel room or at the front desk. It contains a recitation of the heads of state visiting Vietnam, some news about business development, a few ads, and some sports scores.

Information Resources **203**

The *Saigon Times* is a weekly magazine that contains mostly official accounts of the country's economic progress. Note the title of this government-approved publication! Both these local resources are helpful but probably not worth trying to arrange an overseas subscription for at this time.

Given the relative lack of printed matter about the economic developments, one important stop for anyone researching the Vietnam market is FAHASA Publishing Company, Store No. 3, 40 Nguyen Hue, District 1, Ho Chi Minh City (tel: 84-8-225-796). This bookstore contains an excellent bilingual selection of hard-to-find official publications, documents, legal writings, market studies, business and government directories, and United Nations reports concerning Vietnam.

In addition to newspapers and periodicals, another important resource category for the businessperson is the business directory. To find comprehensive sector-by-sector lists of both state-owned and private companies, the best options are the *Ho Chi Minh City Telephone Directory and Yellow Pages* and the *Hanoi Telephone Directory and Yellow Pages*. These are the official phone books given to all telephone customers. Published by Worldcorp Holdings of Singapore and the Post and Telecommunications Ministry of each city, the most valuable part of these color, hardcover volumes is the extensive bilingual listing of foreign and domestic companies in Vietnam. You can order one or both books by contacting Worldcorp Holdings of Singapore, 51 Newton Road, #12-01 Goldhill Plaza, Singapore 1130 (tel: 65-252-3456; fax: 65-252-3310).

Two other useful volumes containing extensive company directories are *Vietnam Opportunities,* published by Annboli Company Ltd. of Hong Kong (tel: 852-523-8638; fax: 852-523-0532), and the *Vietnam Business Yellow Pages* (GPO Box 160, Hong Kong; fax: 852-503-1549).

In addition to all the above resources, a great deal of information can be culled from the newsletters of the

United States and Hong Kong–based organizations listed in chapter 11.

For further details about other documents and pamphlets that provided the research base for this book, please consult the Sources section at the end of this book.

15

Examples of Licensed Projects in Vietnam

There are few secrets in Vietnam when it comes to international business. The State Committee for Cooperation and Investment (SCCI) publishes a complete list of all licensed business projects, including the names and addresses of partners, the nature of the business activity, and the amount of capital scheduled for investment. If the license has since expired or been revoked, that is duly noted as well.

Between 1988 and April 1994, 895 business cooperation, joint venture, and 100% foreign-ownership enterprises had been licensed by Vietnam. Descriptions of all are available in a two-volume publication available for purchase from the SCCI.

The listings are instructive in that they give a concrete picture of foreign business activity in Vietnam to date. I have selected a representative cross-section of the kind of projects approved in 1993.

Project number: 573 (joint venture)
Objective: Build hotel and camping resort at Quang Ninh province
Project name: Hai Ninh Lila Co.
Foreign party: Profit Come Entertainment Development Co. (Hong Kong)
Vietnamese party: Hai Ninh Export Co.
Investment: $2,390,000

Project number: 575 (100% foreign owned)
Objective: Upgrade Defense Ministry guest house to four-star hotel
Project name: Koreana Hotel
Foreign party: Hyosan Development Co. (Korea)
Investment: $3,000,000

Project number: 577 (joint venture)
Objective: Wood processing for export
Project name: N.A.M. Forimex
Foreign party: M.K. Trading (Thailand)
Vietnamese party: Forestrial Products Co. of Nghe An
Investment: $1,771,520

Project number: 580 (100% foreign owned)
Objective: Manufacture guitars
Project name: Emotion Instrument Co.
Foreign party: Emotion Instrument Co. (Taiwan)
Investment: $800,000

Project number: 582 (joint venture)
Objective: Manufacture and distribute high-grade construction materials
Project name: Midovita
Foreign party: Vietnam Australia Building Industry Service (Australia)
Vietnamese party: Brick-Tile Enterprise, Eastern General Co., Dong Nai province
Investment: $1,600,000

Project number: 584 (joint venture)
Objective: Manufacture garments for export

Examples of Licensed Projects in Vietnam

Project name: Daewoo Dong Nai Garment Co.
Foreign party: Daewoo Corp. (Korea)
Vietnamese party: Dong Nai Garment Co.
Investment: $1,700,000

Project number: 587 (joint venture)
Objective: Manufacture high-quality packages
Project name: Hanoi International Packaging Corp.
Foreign party: E. Bridgens and Co. (United Kingdom)
Vietnamese party: Thang Long Import and Export Handicraft Co.
Investment: $1,085,000

Project number: 589 (joint venture)
Objective: Seafood processing
Project name: Swiss Saigon Seafood Co.
Foreign party: Pisciculture Magnerat Co. (Switzerland)
Vietnamese party: Seaprodex
Investment: $3,200,000

Project number: 592 (joint venture)
Objective: Manufacture iron cans and packages
Project name: Tovecan Factory
Foreign party: Ton Yi Industrial Corp. (Taiwan)
Vietnamese party: Vegetexco
Investment: $4,000,000

Project number: 627 (100% foreign owned)
Objective: Manufacture incense, toothpicks, and paper
Project name: WXS Da Nang
Foreign party: Wei Xem Sin Industrial Co. (Taiwan)
Investment: $2,243,000

Project number: 635 (100% foreign owned)
Objective: Manufacture polyester
Project name: Polysindo Vietnam Ltd.

Foreign party: PT Polysindo Eka Perkasa (Indonesia)
Investment: $7,500,000

Project number: 639 (100% foreign owned)
Objective: Manufacture wood furniture
Project name: Nha Trang Handicraft Co.
Foreign party: Imex Pan-Pacific, Buscoro Ventures (Philippines)
Investment: $1,000,000

Project number: 640 (joint venture)
Objective: Construct office building and trade center
Project name: Luks Lavico Co.
Foreign party: Luks Industrial Co. (Hong Kong)
Vietnamese party: Lavico
Investment: $39,388,000

Project number: 648 (100% foreign owned)
Objective: Manufacture steel for construction
Project name: BHP Steel Vietnam
Foreign party: Broken Hill Proprietary Co. (Australia)
Investment: $4,700,000

Project number: 658 (business cooperation contract)
Objective: Provide services for drilling and technology
Project name: Engineering drilling services
Foreign party: International Drilling Fluids (Singapore)
Vietnamese party: Oil Technological Services Co.

Project number: 670 (business cooperation contract)
Objective: Manufacture water filter from anthracite coal
Project name: Water filter contract
Foreign party: Tohkemy Corp. (Japan)

Examples of Licensed Projects in Vietnam

Vietnamese party:	Duong Nhat Investment Co.
Investment:	$1,150,000
Project number:	681 (100% foreign owned)
Objective:	Manufacture scissors and knives
Project name:	Hung Chiea Knives and Scissors
Foreign party:	Hung Chiea Co., Sunnex Fashion Corp. (Taiwan)
Investment:	$500,000
Project number:	684 (joint venture)
Objective:	Build a four-star hotel and provide tourist services
Project name:	Vung Tau-Kiera Festival Resort
Foreign party:	Kiera Construction Ltd. (Australia)
Vietnamese party:	Vietnam Tourist and Trading Center, Vung Tau Tourist Co.
Investment:	$59,177,000
Project number:	686 (100% foreign owned)
Objective:	Construct thermo-power plant to supply electricity
Project name:	Hiep Phuoc Power Co.
Foreign party:	Power Company Ltd. (Hong Kong)
Investment:	$205,000,000
Project number:	691 (100% foreign owned)
Objective:	Grow poultry and animal feed
Project name:	Advance Pharma Vietnam Co.
Foreign party:	Advance Pharma Co., Charoen Pokhand Enterprise (Thailand)
Investment:	$1,513,000
Project number:	726 (joint venture)
Objective:	Build and operate golf course
Project name:	Bochang Dona Tours Golf Country
Foreign party:	Bochang Towals Mfg. Co. (Taiwan)
Vietnamese party:	Dong Nai Tourist Co.
Investment:	$22,729,000

Project number: 732 (joint venture)
Objective: Open international grammar school for expatriate children
Project name: IGS-HCMC
Foreign party: International Grammar School HCM Ltd. (Australia)
Vietnamese party: Saigon Oil Services Co.
Investment: $1,040,000

Project number: 735 (business cooperation contract)
Objective: Oil and gas exploration and exploitation
Project name: Oil Exploration and Exploitation Contract
Foreign party: OMU Exploration (Austria)
Vietnamese party: Petro Vietnam
Investment: $15,000,000

Project number: 780 (100% foreign owned)
Objective: Grow pigs and poultry for food processing
Project name: Top-Mill Animal Farm Enterprise
Foreign party: Top-Mill Enterprise Corp. (Taiwan)
Investment: $8,417,822

Project number: 785 (joint venture)
Objective: Organize tourist excursion by seaplane
Project name: Halong Hydravia
Foreign party: Mr. Denis Menage (France)
Vietnamese party: Hon Gai Tourist and Services Co.
Investment: $130,500

Project number: 792 (joint venture)
Objective: Build and operate sports club in Hanoi
Project name: The Hanoi Club Ltd.
Foreign party: Rising Dragon Ltd. (British Virgin Islands)

Examples of Licensed Projects in Vietnam

    Vietnamese party: Ho Tay Aquatic Development Co.
    Investment: $10,000,000

Project number: 795 (joint venture)
    Objective: Rice milling for export
    Project name: United Grain and Food Milling
    Foreign party: Hasrat Sempurma (Malaysia)
    Vietnamese party: Tien Giang Foodstuff Co.
    Investment: $3,360,038

Project number: 804 (100% foreign owned)
    Objective: Manufacture artificial diamonds
    Project name: Seoul Cubic (VN) Co.
    Foreign party: CT Seoul Cubic Co. (Korea)
    Investment: $300,000

Project number: 807 (joint venture)
    Objective: Manufacture mushrooms and vegetables for export
    Project name: Dalat Fresh Food Co.
    Foreign party: Pactrade Co. (Hong Kong)
    Vietnamese party: Lam Dong Agricultural Product Co.
    Investment: $500,000

Project number: 815 (100% foreign owned)
    Objective: Manufacture pure water
    Project name: Tropical Wave Corp. (VN)
    Foreign party: Tropical Wave Corp. (British Virgin Islands)
    Investment: $1,057,533

Project number: 821 (joint venture)
    Objective: Manufacture instant noodles
    Project name: Vifon Ace Cook Co.
    Foreign party: Ace Cook, Marubeni Corp. (Japan)
    Vietnamese party: Vissan
    Investment: $4,000,000

Project number: 823 (joint venture)
    Objective: Insurance services for foreign-owned capital

Project name: BaoViet-Inchcape Insurance Brokers Ltd.
Foreign party: Inchcape Insurance Holdings (Hong Kong)
Vietnamese party: Bao Viet
Investment: $250,000

Project number: 825 (100% foreign owned)
Objective: Raise shrimp, crab, and seafood for export
Project name: Vinh Linh Co.
Foreign party: Veong Linh Trade Co. (Taiwan)
Investment: $1,000,000

Project number: 830 (joint venture)
Objective: Manufacture aluminum cans
Project name: Carnaud Metal Box (Saigon) Ltd.
Foreign party: CT Carnaud Metal Box Asia Ltd. (Singapore)
Vietnamese party: Saigon Brewery Co.
Investment: $54,000,000

16

LIST OF U.S. FIRMS WITH A PRESENCE IN VIETNAM

One way to gauge initial American interest in the opening of Vietnam is to look at who is the first to go in, either taking the step of setting up an office or displaying products and services. Countless other companies in all fields have also made preparatory moves. Many have sent top executives to visit Vietnam.

U.S. COMPANIES LICENSED TO OPEN REPRESENTATIVE OFFICES

As of mid-1994, the following U.S. companies had opened or been licensed to open representative offices in Vietnam. Firms are listed in the order in which they received their licenses.

1. VATICO (Vietnam Trade and Investment Consulting)
2. Ashta International (consulting)
3. Bank of America
4. Citibank
5. Philip Morris
6. General Electric Technical Services (heavy equipment)
7. Baker Hughes Inc. (oil field services)
8. Baker & McKenzie (law firm)
9. L.A. Land Resources (construction)
10. Otis Elevator
11. VIIC (Vietnam Information and Consulting)
12. IBM
13. American Service Co. (consulting)
14. Spivey International (consulting)
15. Connell Bros. Co. (trading)
16. American International Group (insurance)
17. Gemrusa (precious stones)
18. Manolis and Company Asia (real estate)
19. Carrier Corp. (refrigeration equipment)
20. Caterpillar World Trading (earth-moving machinery)
21. H&N Fish Co.
22. Indochina Partners Ltd. (trading)
23. ARF Overseas Management Corp. (consulting)
24. Russin & Vecchi (law firm)
25. American Trading Corp. (trading)
26. Deloitte Touche Tohmatsu (accounting)
27. Digital Equipment (computers)
28. American President Lines (shipping)

List of U.S. Firms with a Vietnam Presence

    29. DuPont Far East Inc. (chemicals)
    30. Motorola Inc. (telecommunications)
    31. International Direct Marketing (marketing)
    32. Kodak Thailand Ltd. (film)
    33. Technomic Consultants International (consulting)
    34. Pacific Southeast Asia Inc. (consulting)

[Source: *Los Angeles Times*]

LIST OF COMPANIES EXHIBITING AT VIETNAMERICA EXPO '94

On April 21–24, 1994, the first exhibition of American companies and products since the lifting of the U.S. trade embargo took place in Hanoi. The following is a list of companies and organizations participating.

1. American Worldwide Trading, Hackettstown, N.J.
   Tel: 908-850-3328
   Fax: 908-850-1760
   Consumer products

2. Ampolmed Inc., Fresno, Calif.
   Tel: 209-456-4088
   Fax: 209-456-3662
   Medical equipment

3. Apcie Inc., Montebello, Calif.
   Tel: 213-720-1519
   Fax: 213-726-0243
   Distributor of power gas engines

4. Azon Keuffel and Esser, Johnson City, N.Y.
   Tel: 607-797-2366
   Fax: 607-797-4506
   Coated papers, films, maps for design, architecture, and construction

5. Carrier Corporation, Singapore
   Tel: 65-337-3344
   Fax: 65-338-6163
   Air conditioning, heating, and refrigeration equipment

6. California State University, Fullerton, Calif.
   Campus in state university system

7. Culligan International, Northbrook, Ill.
   Tel: 708-205-5922
   Fax: 708-205-6040
   Water treatment

8. DeMatteis Construction, Elmont, N.Y.
   Tel: 516-285-5500
   Fax: 516-285-8248
   Construction management

9. De-Sta-Co, Bangkok, Thailand
   Tel: 662-326-0812
   Fax: 662-326-0580
   Toggle clamps and other industrial work-holding devices

10. Digital Equipment, Hong Kong
    Tel: 852-805-3111
    Fax: 852-805-4200
    Computers and information systems

11. Echostar International, Singapore
    Tel: 65-779-4166
    Fax: 65-779-6051
    Satellite television systems

12. Figgie Fire Protection Systems, Charlottesville, Va.
    Tel: 804-974-4102
    Fax: 804-978-1922
    Fire protection equipment

13. Fleetguard International, Nashville, Tenn.
    Tel: 615-367-0040
    Fax: 615-399-3650
    Diesel engines and filtration devices

14. Fluke Corporation, Everett, Wa.
    Tel: 206-356-5512
    Fax: 206-356-5116
    Electronic test and measurement equipment
15. GE Appliances, Hanoi
    Tel: 844-251-017
    Fax: 844-250-511
    Major appliances
16. GE Industrial and Power Systems, Hanoi
    Tel: 844-251-017
    Fax: 844-250-511
    Generators and power delivery equipment
17. GE Lighting, Hanoi
    Tel: 844-251-017
    Fax: 844-250-511
    Lighting for consumer, commercial, and industrial markets
18. GE Transportation Systems, Hanoi
    Tel: 844-251-017
    Fax: 844-250-511
    Locomotives, motors, generators, and parts
19. Gillette, Shah Alam, Malaysia
    Tel: 603-559-2116
    Fax: 603-550-4762
    Consumer products
20. HECNY Transportation, Inglewood, Calif.
    Tel: 310-338-3333
    Fax: 310-338-3345
    International freight forwarder and custom broker
21. IBM Vietnam, Hanoi
    Tel: 844-226-316
    Fax: 844-226-320
    Computers
22. International Bridge Systems, Hanoi
    Tel: 844-259-675
    Fax: 844-250-421

23. Ingersoll Rand Southeast Asia, Singapore
    Tel: 65-860-6716
    Fax: 65-861-6617
    Construction and mining machinery
24. Jardine-Radix International, Los Angeles, Calif.
    Tel: 310-338-2400
    Fax: 310-417-5031
    International freight forwarder and custom broker
25. KFC International, Bangkok
    Tel: 662-251-8080
    Fax: 254-3260
    Fried chicken restaurant chain
26. Kraft General Foods, Rye Brook, N.Y.
    Tel: 914-335-1542
    Fax: 914-335-1522
    Food products
27. Kulthorn International, Bangkok
    Tel: 662-282-2151
    Fax: 662-280-1444
    Compressors, electric motors, and thermostats
28. Mosley Machinery, Winston-Salem, N.C.
    Tel: 910-750-0751
    Fax: 910-750-0831
    Solid waste disposal; recycling and scrap-processing systems
29. Otis Elevator, Singapore
    Tel: 65-337-3344
    Fax: 75-339-6163
    Elevators, escalators, and moving walkways
30. Pepsico Foods International, Bangkok
    Tel: 662-258-9058
    Fax: 662-258-9030
    Snack foods
31. Pizza Hut, Bangkok
    Tel: 662-258-9058

Fax: 662-258-9030
Restaurants

32. Pepsi Cola, Bangkok
Tel: 662-258-9058
Fax: 662-258-9030
Soft drinks

33. Phamatech, San Diego, Calif.
Tel: 619-689-0640
Fax: 619-689-9817
Medical diagnostic devices

34. Port of Oakland, Calif.
Tel: 510-272-1100
Fax: 310-272-1172
International port

35. TD & T/Microsoft, Hanoi
Tel: 844-243-663
Fax: 844-260-723
Microsoft products

36. The Gannon Companies, St. Louis, Mo.
Tel: 314-576-9600
Fax: 314-434-0582
Real estate development, construction, travel, and product distribution

37. The Jel Sert Company, West Chicago, Ill.
Tel: 708-231-7590
Fax: 708-231-3993
Fruit drinks and powdered drink mixes

38. Trans Technology, Singapore
Tel: 65-296-1919
Fax: 65-296-0055
Hand tools, pumps, and welding equipment

39. Usvina Corporation, San Diego, Calif.
Tel: 619-535-9679
Fax: 619-535-0107

Communications systems; metal and dental equipment

40. Vector Venture Corporation, Sparks, Nev.
    Tel: 702-331-5524
    Fax: 702-331-5527
    Water purification

41. Vietnam Investment Information and Consulting, San Diego, Calif.
    Tel: 619-277-5580
    Fax: 619-277-9411
    Vietnamerica Expo '94 sponsor

42. York International, York, Pa
    Tel: 717-771-6177
    Fax: 717-771-6843
    Air conditioning and refrigeration equipment

43. Willert Home Products, St. Louis, Mo.
    Tel: 314-772-2822
    Fax: 314-772-3506
    Home products

44. Wirtgen America, Nashville, Tenn.
    Tel: 615-391-0600
    Fax: 615-391-0791
    Road rehabilitation and maintenance equipment

17

DOING BUSINESS IN VIETNAM: THE BOTTOM LINE

Novelist and philosopher Ayn Rand, whose seminal work *Atlas Shrugged* weighed in at well over a thousand pages, liked to tell the story about the time she was asked at a university lecture whether she was able to state the essence of her philosophy while standing on one foot. "I did so as follows," she boasted: "Politics: capitalism. Ethics: self-interest. Metaphysics: objective reality. Epistemology: reason."

Summarizing the essence of the opportunities and challenges of doing business in Vietnam while standing on one foot is no easy task, either—especially because the market is at that stage when most of us are simply trying to get our feet wet!

Nonetheless, consider as food for thought the following ten myths and ten realities about this dynamic, rapidly changing market.

Ten Myths about Doing Business in Vietnam

1. The Vietnamese market is better suited for large multinational companies than it is for entrepreneurs.
2. Vietnam is interested only in big infrastructure projects.
3. Vietnam is too poor and too small to be a market of consequence.
4. Vietnam is a place where you can operate at low cost and turn a quick profit.
5. You can't get much accomplished in Vietnam without paying bribes.
6. Vietnamese harbor anger and enmity toward Americans because of the war.
7. Economic liberalization means that political pluralism and individual rights will soon follow.
8. Hiring overseas Vietnamese or joining with them as partners will hurt you more than help you.
9. Vietnamese believe that the foreign way is the best way and are willing to play the role of obedient pupil.
10. All the good opportunities are taken. It's too late for Americans.

Ten Realities about Doing Business in Vietnam

1. Vietnam is a large market of 71 million people, the world's thirteenth most populous nation.

2. Vietnam is strategically located in the center of the world's most dynamic growth region—Southeast Asia.
3. Vietnam is endowed with natural resources such as oil, timber, and productive farmland. It has an abundant supply of cheap yet well-educated and hardworking labor.
4. Vietnam is in the midst of a radical transformation from a centrally planned socialist economy to a market economy that has produced both substantial economic improvement and opportunities for international business.
5. The lifting of the U.S. trade embargo and related policy developments, such as renewed international aid and lending, have provided further positive momentum to help Vietnam complete the transformation to a market economy.
6. Major customers and average urban consumers alike identify positively with many U.S. brand names and have a preference for American products. Rising income levels mean that increasing numbers of Vietnamese can afford these products.
7. Although U.S. companies lost deals because of the embargo, the market is young enough and the identification with American business strong enough that the best opportunities are yet to be realized.
8. Starting small, choosing a good partner, being flexible, and exercising patience are the qualities required for success and profits in Vietnam, making the market ideal for creative entrepreneurs.
9. Establishing relationships, gaining knowledge of the culture, and appreciating the many admirable qualities of the Vietnamese people will enhance

your chances for success and satisfaction in your business endeavors.

10. Vietnam is one of the last frontiers for international businesspeople who wish to experience the challenge and excitement of a new, emerging market as it struggles to reinvent itself in time for the twenty-first century.

A

VIETNAM'S FOREIGN INVESTMENT LAW AND KEY AMENDMENTS

For international businesses, the December 1987 Law on Foreign Investment in Vietnam is the seminal document signaling Vietnam's open-door policy to the world. Along with subsequent amendments and implementing regulations, it is worth studying in detail. Here you will find official definitions of various forms of doing business as well as tax rates and concessions. The following is a translation of the law, including excerpts from key amendments and regulations as provided by the State Committee for Cooperation and Investment.

National Assembly
Socialist Republic of Vietnam
Hanoi, 29 December, 1987

Law on Foreign Investment in Vietnam

In order to expand economic cooperation with foreign countries, develop a national economy and increase exports on the basis of the efficient exploitation of natural resources, labor, and all other potential of the country;

In accordance with articles 16, 21, and 83 of the Constitution of the Socialist Republic of Vietnam;

This law makes provisions for investment by foreign organizations and individuals in the Socialist Republic of Vietnam.

CHAPTER I
General Provisions

Article 1

The State of the Socialist Republic of Vietnam welcomes and encourages foreign organizations and individuals to invest capital and technology in Vietnam on the basis of respect for the independence and sovereignty of Vietnam, observance of Vietnamese laws, equality and mutual benefit.

The State of Vietnam guarantees the ownership of invested capital and other rights of foreign organizations and individuals, and provides favorable conditions and simple procedures for investment in Vietnam.

Article 2

In this Law, the following terms shall have the meanings ascribed to them hereunder:

1. *Foreign party* means one or more foreign individuals or legal economic entities.

2. *Vietnamese party* means one or more Vietnamese legal economic entities. Vietnamese individuals may contribute capital to Vietnamese legal economic entities to form the Vietnamese party for the purposes of business cooperation with a foreign party.

3. *Foreign investment* means direct investment in Vietnam, in accordance with provisions of this Law, of foreign currency or such assets as may be approved by the Vietnamese Government by foreign organizations and individuals for the purposes of contractual business cooperation, or for the establishment of a joint venture enterprise or an enterprise with one hundred percent foreign owned capital.

4. *The two parties* means the Vietnamese party and the foreign party.

5. *A business cooperation contract* means a contract in writing for business cooperation signed by a foreign party and a Vietnamese party.

6. *A joint venture contract* means a contract in writing for the establishment of a joint venture enterprise signed by a foreign party and a Vietnamese party.

7. *Contributed capital* means the capital contributed by a foreign or Vietnamese party which forms part of the capital of a joint venture enterprise but does not include any loans or other credits provided to the joint venture enterprise.

8. *A reinvestment* means the retention of any part of the profits for the purposes of addition to an investor's initially contributed capital or for new investment in any of the forms provided for in article 4 of this Law.

9. *Prescribed capital* means the initial capital of a joint venture enterprise as stated in its charter.

10. *A joint venture enterprise* means an enterprise jointly set up in Vietnam by a foreign and a Vietnamese party, pursuant to a joint venture contract or to an agreement which has been concluded between the

Government of the Socialist Republic of Vietnam and a foreign government.

11. *An enterprise with one hundred percent foreign owned capital* means an enterprise the capital of which is one hundred percent owned by foreign organizations or individuals and which is authorized by the Government of the Socialist Republic of Vietnam to be established in Vietnam.

12. *An enterprise with foreign owned capital* means either a joint venture enterprise or an enterprise with one hundred percent foreign owned capital.

Article 3

Foreign organizations and individuals may invest in Vietnam in any sectors of its national economy.

The State of Vietnam encourages foreign organizations and individuals to invest in the following sectors:

1. Implementation of major economic programs, export orientation production, and import substitution.
2. The use of high technology, skilled labor, and concentrated investment in the exploitation and exhaustive utilization of potential resources and in the increasing of the production capacity of existing factories.
3. Production which is labor intensive and uses existing materials and natural resources available in Vietnam.
4. Building of infrastructure projects.
5. Foreign currency earning services such as tourism, ship repairing, airports, and sea ports and other services.

A detailed list of the areas in which foreign investment is encouraged will be published by the State body in charge of foreign investment.

Chapter II

Forms of Investment

Article 4

Foreign organizations and individuals may invest in any of the following forms:
1. Contractual business cooperation.
2. Joint venture enterprises or corporation, generally called joint venture enterprise.
3. An enterprise with one hundred percent foreign owned capital.

Article 5

A foreign party and a Vietnamese party may, pursuant to a business cooperation contract, enter into production sharing or other cooperation.

The parties shall agree upon and expressly state, in a business cooperation contract, the objects and nature of the business, together with details of their respective rights, obligations, and responsibilities and the relationship between them.

Article 6

Two parties may establish a joint venture enterprise. Each joint venture enterprise shall be a legal entity which is subject to the laws of Vietnam.

Article 7

The foreign party to a joint venture enterprise may make its contribution to prescribed capital in:
1. Foreign currency.
2. Plant, buildings, equipment, machinery, tools, components, and spare parts.
3. Patents, technical know-how, technological processes, and technical services.

The Vietnamese party in a joint venture may make its contribution to prescribed capital in:

1. Vietnamese currency.
2. Natural resources.
3. Building materials, fixtures, and furnishings.
4. The right to use land, water surface or sea surface.
5. Plant, buildings, equipment, machinery, tools, components, and spare parts.
6. The supervision of construction and commissioning of plant, patents, technical know-how, technological processes, and technical services.

The two parties may agree to contribute to prescribed capital in forms other than those described above.

Article 8

There shall be no ceiling to the proportion of contribution made by a foreign party to the prescribed capital of a joint venture enterprise. The minimum contribution shall be thirty percent of the total prescribed capital contributed by the parties.

The value of the capital contribution made by each party shall be assessed on the basis of international market prices and expressed in the charter of the joint venture enterprises in either Vietnamese currency or other currency as agreed upon.

Article 9

All assets of the joint venture enterprise shall be insured by a Vietnamese insurance company or other insurance company as agreed upon by both parties.

Article 10

The two parties shall share the profits and bear the risks associated with a joint venture enterprise in accordance with the proportions of their respective contributions to its capital.

Appendix A

Article 11

In order to maintain foreign currency balance in a joint venture enterprise the two parties shall agree upon the proportion of products to be allocated respectively for the purposes of export from and sale in Vietnam. All foreign currency earned from exports and other sources shall, at least, be sufficient to meet all foreign currency requirements of the joint venture enterprise so as to ensure its normal operation and to protect the interests of the foreign party.

Article 12

The body in charge of a joint venture enterprise shall be its board of management.

Each party to a joint venture enterprise shall appoint members to the board of management in proportion to its contribution to the capital of the enterprise provided, however, that each party has at least two members appointed to the board.

The chairman of the board shall be appointed in accordance with the agreement of the two parties.

The general director and deputy general directors shall be appointed by the board of management to conduct the day-to-day business of the joint venture enterprise and shall be responsible to it for the operation of the joint venture enterprise.

Either the general director or the first deputy general director of the board of management shall be a Vietnamese citizen.

Article 13

All principal matters which relate of the organization and operation of the joint venture, namely its business objectives, business planning, and key personnel, shall be determined by a unanimous decision of the board of management.

Article 14

Foreign organizations and individuals may establish in Vietnam enterprises with one hundred percent foreign owned capital, in which case they shall assume full responsibility for the management of the enterprise, be subject to the control of the State body in charge of foreign investment, and be entitled to enjoy the rights and be liable to carry out all obligations stated in the investment license.

Each enterprise with one hundred percent foreign owned capital shall be a legal entity which is subject to the laws of Vietnam.

Article 15

The duration of an enterprise with foreign owned capital shall not exceed twenty years. Where necessary, the duration may be extended for a longer period.

Article 16

Vietnamese citizens shall be given priority in the recruitment of personnel for an enterprise with foreign owned capital.

Where advanced technical qualifications are required and Vietnamese persons having those qualifications are not available, the enterprise may recruit foreign personnel.

The rights and obligations of the Vietnamese employees working in an enterprise with foreign owned capital shall be provided for labor contracts.

The salaries and allowances of Vietnamese employees shall be denominated in a foreign currency by payable in Vietnamese currency.

Article 17

An enterprise with foreign owned capital shall open bank accounts in both Vietnamese currency and foreign currency with the Bank of Foreign Trade of Vietnam or with such branches of foreign banks established in Vietnam as may be approved by the State Bank of Vietnam.

Article 18

An enterprise with foreign owned capital shall keep its books of account in accordance with conventional international principles and standards approved by the Ministry of Finance of the Socialist Republic of Vietnam and shall be subject to audit under the supervision and control of the financial bodies of Vietnam.

Article 19

The establishment, transfer of capital, and dissolution of an enterprise with foreign-owned capital shall take place in accordance with its charter and in compliance with Vietnamese laws.

An enterprise with foreign owned capital shall have the status of a legal entity from the date of registration of its charter or by the State body in charge of foreign investment.

CHAPTER III
Investment Guarantee Measures

Article 20

The Government of the Socialist Republic of Vietnam guarantees that a foreign investment which, or individual who, invests in Vietnam shall be treated fairly and equitably.

Article 21

The capital and assets invested in Vietnam by foreign organizations or individuals shall not be requisitioned or expropriated through administrative measures. An enterprise with foreign owned capital shall not be nationalized.

Article 22

Foreign organizations and individuals investing in Vietnam shall have the right to transfer abroad:

1. Their share of profits derived from business operations.
2. Any payments due as a result of provision of technology or services.

3. The principal of any loan made in the course of a business operation together with interest thereon.
4. Their invested capital.
5. Other sums of money and assets lawfully owned by them.

Article 23

Foreigners working in Vietnam for enterprises with foreign-owned capital or performing business cooperation contracts shall, following payment of income taxes as stipulated by Vietnamese law, be authorized to transfer abroad their incomes in accordance with the foreign exchange control regulations of Vietnam.

Article 24

The conversion of Vietnamese currency into foreign currency shall be effected at the official exchange rate published by the State Bank of Vietnam.

Article 25

Resolution of any dispute between the two parties to a business cooperation contract or a joint venture contract, or between either a joint venture enterprise or enterprise with one hundred percent foreign owned capital and any Vietnamese economic organization or other enterprise with foreign owned capital, shall be attempted by negotiation and conciliation.

If, however, the two parties to a dispute fail to agree, then the dispute shall be referred to a Vietnamese economic arbitration body or other arbitration or judicial body as may be agreed.

Chapter IV

Rights and Obligations of Foreign Organizations and Individuals

Article 26

Enterprises with foreign owned capital and foreign parties to business cooperation contracts shall be liable to pay profits tax at a rate of between fifteen percent and twenty five percent of profits earned.

In the case of profits derived from oil and gas and certain other valuable and rare resources, profits tax shall be levied at a higher rate in accordance with accepted international practice.

Article 27

Depending on the sector of the economy in which the investment is made, the scale of capital contribution, the volume of exports, and the nature and duration of the business, a joint venture enterprise may be exempted by the State body in charge of foreign investment from payment of profits tax for a maximum period of two years commencing from the first profit-making year and, further, it may be allowed a fifty percent reduction of profits tax for a maximum period of the two successive years.

Operating losses incurred by a joint venture enterprise in any year may be carried forward to the following year and set off against the profits of that year. Any losses remaining after such set off may be carried forward on the same basis for up to five successive years.

Article 28

In special cases where encouragement of investment is needed, a reduction of profits tax may be extended for a period longer than that provided for in article 27 of this Law.

Article 29

An enterprise with foreign owned capital and a foreign party to a business cooperation contract shall pay rent for the use of land, water surface, and sea surface in Vietnam. They shall pay a royalty in the case of exploitation of natural resources.

Article 30

After payment of its profits tax, a joint venture enterprise shall appropriate five percent of the remaining profits to establishing a reserve fund. Such reserve fund shall be limited to twenty-five percent of the prescribed capital of the enterprise. The percentage of profits which shall be used to set up other funds shall be determined by agreement between the two parties and stated in the charter of the enterprise.

Article 31

An enterprise with foreign owned capital shall, in accordance with the laws of Vietnam, pay to the State Treasury of Vietnam the sums required for social insurance of the employees of the enterprise.

Article 32

Where any foreign organization or individuals reinvest part of their share of the profits, they shall receive a refund from the tax authorities of the amount of profits tax already paid on that part of those profits.

Article 33

Upon transfer of their profits abroad, the foreign organizations or individuals concerned shall pay tax at a rate of between five percent and ten percent of the transferred profits.

In special cases where encouragement of investment is needed, exemption from, or reduction of, the tax may be granted by the State body in charge of foreign investment.

Article 34

Enterprises with foreign owned capital shall, during their operations, take all precautions necessary for protection of the environment.

Appendix A

Article 35

Products exported or imported by either an enterprise with foreign owned capital or the parties to a business cooperation contract shall be subject to export and import duty in accordance with the Law on Export and Import Duties on Commercial Goods.

In special cases where encouragement of investment is needed the State body in charge of foreign investment may grant exemption from, or reduction of, the export of import duty.

Chapter V

State Body in Charge of Foreign Investment

Article 36

The State body of the Government of the Socialist Republic of Vietnam in charge of foreign investment is vested with the overall responsibility for matters relating to the investment activities of foreign organizations and individuals in Vietnam.

The State body in charge of foreign investment shall have the following powers and duties:

1. To assist foreign and Vietnamese parties in the negotiation and conclusion of business cooperation and joint venture contracts, to assist foreign organizations and individuals in the establishments in Vietnam of enterprises with one hundred percent foreign owned capital, and assist in the resolution of all other matters at the request of those organizations and individuals.

2. To consider and approve business cooperation and joint venture contracts, authorize the establishment by foreign organizations and individuals of enterprises with one hundred percent foreign owned capital, and approve the charters of those enterprises with foreign owned capital.

3. To determine and grant preferential treatment to enterprises with foreign owned capital and to parties to business cooperation contracts.
4. To monitor and supervise the performance of business cooperation and joint venture contracts and the operation of enterprises with one hundred percent foreign owned capital.
5. To analyze the economic activities of enterprises with foreign owned capital.

Article 37

An application for approval of a business cooperation contract or a joint venture contract, the establishment of an enterprise with one hundred percent foreign owned capital or for investment incentives shall be submitted to the state body in charge of foreign investment by the two parties or, alternatively, by the foreign investing organization or individual concerned. The application shall be accompanied by the business cooperation or joint venture contract, the charter of the joint venture enterprise or enterprise with one hundred percent foreign owned capital, a study of the economic and technical feasibility of the project and such other documents as may be required by the State body in charge of foreign investment.

Article 38

The application shall be considered by the State body in charge of foreign investment and its decision shall be communicated to the parties concerned within three months from the date of its receipt of the application. Approval shall be communicated by the issue of an investment license.

Chapter VI
Final Provisions

Article 39

In accordance with the principles provided in this Law, the Government of the Socialist Republic of Vietnam shall enact regulations which provide for the creation of favorable conditions for overseas Vietnamese to invest in Vietnam as their contribution to national reconstruction.

Article 40

The Government of the Socialist Republic of Vietnam may, in accordance with the principles provided in this Law, conclude with foreign governments, agreements on cooperation and investment which are consistent with the economic relationship between them.

Article 41

The Regulations on Foreign Investment in the Socialist Republic of Vietnam issued with Decree No. 115-CQ dated 18 April 1977 together with all other provisions inconsistent with this Law are hereby repealed.

Article 42

The Council of Ministers of the Socialist Republic of Vietnam shall issue detailed provisions for the implementation of this Law.

This Law was approved by the Legislature VIII of the National Assembly of the Socialist Republic of Vietnam at its 2nd Session on 29 December 1987.

President of the National Assembly
LE QUANG DAO

National Assembly
Socialist Republic of Vietnam
Hanoi, 30 June 1990

Excerpts From Law on Amendment of and Addition to a Number of Articles of the Law on Foreign Investment n Vietnam

Article 1

Articles 2, 3, 5, 6, 7, 8, 10, 11, 12, 16, 25, 27, 29, 30, and 37 are amended and added to as follows:

Clauses 2, 4, 5, 6, and 10 of article 2 are amended and added to as follows:

> 2. *Vietnamese party* means one or more Vietnamese legal economic entities operating in an economic sector.
> 4. *The two sides* means the Vietnamese party and the foreign party.

Multi-party means a Vietnamese party and more than one foreign party, or a foreign party and more than one Vietnamese party, or more than one Vietnamese party and more than one foreign party....

The following clause is added to the end of article 3:

Vietnamese private economic organizations shall be permitted to enter into business cooperation contracts with foreign organizations and individuals, in the economic sectors, and subject to the conditions stipulated by the Council of Ministers.

Article 5 is amended and added to and now is as follows:

Any two or more parties may, pursuant to a business cooperation contract, enter into production sharing or other cooperation.

The two sides shall agree upon, and expressly state in the business cooperation contract, the objects and nature of the business, their respective rights, obligations, and responsibilities, and the relationship between them....

Article 8 is amended and added to and now is as follows:

There shall be no ceiling to the proportion of contribution made by a foreign party to the prescribed capital of a joint venture enterprise. The minimum proportion of contribution shall be thirty percent of the total prescribed capital contributed by the two sides.

In the case of a multi-party joint venture enterprise, the minimum proportion of capital contribution to be made by each Vietnamese party shall be determined by the Council of Ministers....

Paragraph 4 of article 16 is amended and added to and now is as follows:

The salaries and allowances of the Vietnamese employees shall be paid from the bank account of the joint venture enterprise in Vietnamese or foreign currency.

Paragraph 1 of article 27 is amended and added to and now is as follows:

Depending on the sector of the economy in which the investment is made, the location of investment, the scale of capital contribution, the volume of exports, the volume of substitutions for imports of those products which are not as yet produced or not produced in sufficient quantity in Vietnam, the nature and duration of the business, a joint venture enterprise may be exempted by the State body in charge of foreign investment from payment of profits tax for a maximum period of two years commencing from the first profit-making year and it may be allowed a fifty percent reduction of profits tax for a maximum period of the two successive years....

This Law was approved by the Legislature VIII of the National Assembly of the Socialist Republic of Vietnam at its 7th Session on 30 June 1990.

President of the National Assembly
LE QUANG DAO

National Assembly
Socialist Republic of Vietnam
Hanoi, 23 December 1992

Excerpts From Law on Amendment of and Addition to a Number of Articles of the Law on Foreign Investment in Vietnam

Article 1

Article 2 is amended and added to as follows:

a. Clause 2 is amended and added to and now is as follows:

Vietnamese party may consist of one or more economic organizations of any economic sector.

b. The following clauses are added to article 2:

13. *Export Processing Zone* means an industrial zone specializing in export-oriented production, carrying out the services for export-oriented production and export activities; comprising one or more enterprises, with a specific geographical boundary; and set up by the Government of Vietnam.

14. *Export Processing Enterprise* means an enterprise which shall be established within the Export Processing Zone.

15. *Construction-Business-Transfer Contract* means the documents signed by the foreign organization or individual with the authorized state agency of Vietnam to build an infrastructure project; then manage and exploit the project in a certain period; upon its export, the foreign organization or individual shall transfer the project, without any condition attached, to the Vietnamese Government....

Article 15 is amended and added to and now is as follows:

The duration of an enterprise with foreign invested capital shall be determined upon each project, but shall not exceed fifty years. On the basis of the Standing Committee of the National Assembly's decision, the Government shall extend the duration for each project, but the maximum period shall not exceed seventy years.

Article 17 is amended and added to and now is as follows:

An enterprise with foreign owned capital may open bank accounts in both Vietnamese currency and foreign currency with Vietnamese banks or joint venture banks or branches of foreign banks located in Vietnam.

In special cases, an enterprise with foreign owned capital may open borrowing account at overseas banks and subject to conditions stipulated by the State Bank of Vietnam.

Article 19a and 19b are added to as follows:

Article 19a:

Foreign economic organizations and individuals may invest in export processing zones in any of the forms as stipulated in article 4 of this Law.

Vietnamese business enterprises of any economic sector are permitted to cooperate with foreign organizations which and individuals who invest in export processing zones in any of the forms stipulated in clauses 1, 2 of article 4 of this Law to establish an enterprise with one hundred percent of its own capital.

Goods exchanged between enterprises in Vietnam's market and export processing enterprises shall be regarded as exports and imports and subject to the Regulations on export-import activities....

Article 19b:

Foreign organizations and individuals investing in Vietnam to build infrastructure projects, may sign Construction-Business-Transfer Contracts with authorized agencies of Vietnam. Foreign economic organizations and individuals shall be entitled to enjoy the rights and liable to carry out all obligations stated in the contract....

The following is added to the end of article 27:

In special cases where encouragement of investment is needed the Government shall decide to give preferential treatment to an enterprise with one hundred percent foreign owned capital as stated in paragraphs 1 and 2 of this article.

Article 35a is added as follows:

Export processing enterprises shall be entitled to:

1. Be exempt from payment of duties for goods exported from and imported into the export processing zone:

2. Enjoy preferential taxes as stated in article 28, article 33 of this Law. The Government shall stipulate specific taxes for each export processing enterprise....

This Law was approved by the Legislature IX of the National Assembly of the Socialist Republic of Vietnam at its 2nd Session on 23 December, 1992.

President of the National Assembly
NONG DUC MANH

Appendix A

Decree of the Government
The Socialist Republic of Vietnam
Hanoi, 16 April 1993

Excerpts from Regulations in Detail for the Implementation of the Law on Foreign Investment in Vietnam

CHAPTER I
General Provisions

Article 1

This Decree concretizes the Foreign Investment Law and regulates in detail direct investment operations of foreigners in Vietnam....

Article 2

Terms used in this Decree shall be understood as follows:

1. *The legal capital of a foreign invested enterprise* is the initial capital of the enterprise, and is prescribed in the chapter of the enterprise. Loan capital is not included in the legal capital of the enterprise;
2. *The investment capital* is the capital needed to carry out the investment project, and it includes the legal capital and loan capital.

Article 3

The objects of regulation of the Foreign Investment Law are specified hereunder:

1. Vietnamese economic organizations of all economic components including:

- State-run businesses;
- Cooperatives;
- Businesses established following the Company Law;
- Private businesses established following the Law on Private Businesses;

2. Foreign economic organizations and individuals directly investing in Vietnam;
3. Enterprises with foreign investment capital;
4. State agencies which sign and implement Building-Operating-Transferring contracts (B.O.T.);
5. Vietnamese residents abroad making direct investments in Vietnam or joining capital with Vietnamese economic organizations to constitute the Vietnamese partner for investment cooperation with a foreign partner. In both cases, they shall enjoy favorable conditions separately provided for....

CHAPTER II
Contractual Business Cooperation

Article 8

1. A business cooperation contract is a document signed by two partners or several partners (referred to briefly as the partners) with a view to jointly conducting one or more business operations in Vietnam on the basis of mutual allocation of responsibilities and distribution of business results without creating any other new judicial person;

   Commercial contracts and economic contracts in the nature of goods exchange, such as delivery of raw materials in return for finished products, purchase of equipment with deferred payment in products, etc. are not within the scope of this Decree.

2. The term of a business cooperation contract shall be agreed upon between the partners in keeping with the nature and object of the business, and shall be approved by the State Committee for Cooperation and Investment.
3. A business cooperation contract must be signed by duly authorized representatives of the contracting partners.

Article 9

An application to the State Committee for Cooperation and Investment for issuance of a business license shall be signed by contracting partners and enclosed with the following documents:

1. The business cooperation contract;
2. Necessary information relating to the partners such as the charter of the company or the legal status of the individual as a partner of the contract, and the financial capacities of the partners.
3. A demonstration of the economic technical base of the contract.

Article 10

A business cooperation contract must comprise the following contents:

1. Nationalities, addresses and duly authorized representatives of the partners;
2. A description of the business activities;
3. A descriptive list, quantity and quality of the main equipment and materials; specification, quantity and quality of the products; the ratio of domestic and foreign consumption; the ration of foreign currency and Vietnamese currency to be collected. In case of the production of import substitution goods, the mode of payment must be expressly stated;
4. The obligations and rights of the partners, method for determination of business results, conditions of

assignment of their respective obligations and rights under the contract;

5. The term of the contract, responsibilities of the partners in the execution of the contract, amendments to and termination of the contract;
6. The procedure for settlement of disputes between the partners arising from the execution of the contract;
7. Validity of the contract.

Article 11

1. Within three months upon the receipt of the application for issuance of a business license, the State Committee for Cooperation and Investment shall notify the partners of its decision;
2. In case the State Committee for Cooperation and Investment requests the partners to supply additional documents or amend a number of provisions of the contract, the former shall have to send its requests to the latter within one month from the date of receipt of the application for issuance of a business license....

Article 12

A business cooperation contract shall not become effective until it is granted a business license by the State Committee for Cooperation and Investment. Within 30 days from the date of receipt of the business license, the partners shall have to publish it in the central newspaper or the local newspaper with the following contents:

- Names, addresses, and representatives of the partners;
- Description of business activities;
- Representatives of the partners before Vietnamese court and state agency;
- Term of the business cooperation contract and date of receipt of the business license....

Article 14

In case the contracting partners agree to extend the term of the contract, they shall have to file an application to this effect to the State Committee for Cooperation and Investment at least six months prior to the expiry of the contract. Within 15 days upon the receipt of the application, the State Committee for Cooperation and Investment shall notify the partners of its decision....

Article 17

Each partner of the business cooperation contract shall:

1. Ensure full payment of all the taxes that are due: the foreign partner pays taxes in accordance with the Foreign Investment Law; the Vietnamese partner fulfills tax obligations in compliance with laws on taxation applied to domestic businesses;
2. Be responsible for its own activities before the law of the Socialist Republic of Vietnam.

Article 18

1. The partners shall clear the contract in accordance with regulations stated in the business cooperation contract. The duration for executing the clearance of the contract shall not exceed six months since the expiry of the contract or since the decision to terminate the contract. In necessary cases, this duration may be extended for longer but it shall not exceed one year;
2. All expenses for the clearance of the contract shall be borne by the partners, and shall be liquidated in priority, in comparison with other liabilities;
3. Other liabilities shall be settled in the following priority order:
    - Wages and other labor insurance expenses the partners still owe the laborers.
    - Taxes and their equivalent that are due to the Vietnamese Government.

- Loans (including interest).
- Other liquidations.

Chapter III
Joint Venture

Article 19

1. A joint venture is established in Vietnam on the basis of a joint venture contract signed by a Vietnamese partner or several Vietnamese partners and a foreign partner or several foreign partners....

2. A joint venture is established following the form of the limited liability company and is a Vietnamese juridical person; each joint venture partner shall bear the responsibility to the other partner to the joint venture and to the third partner with regards to its contribution of legal capital;

3. A joint venture shall operate on the principle of independent economic accounting on the basis of the joint venture contract and the charter of the joint venture in conformity with the investment license and the law of the Socialist Republic of Vietnam;

4. A joint venture is formally established upon issuance of an investment license and the certificate of registration of its charter by the State Committee for Cooperation and Investment.

Article 20

An application submitted to the State Committee for Cooperation and Investment for issuance of an investment license must be signed by all joint venture partners and be accompanied with the following documents:

1. A joint venture contract;
2. The charter of the joint venture;

Appendix A

3. Necessary information relating to the legal status and financial capacity of joint venture partners;
4. An economic-technical description.

Article 21

A joint venture contract shall contain the following main items:

1. Nationalities, addresses and authorized representatives of joint venture partners;
2. Name, address and business activities of the joint venture;
3. The investment capital, the legal capital, the capital contribution of each partner, the mode and progress rate of capital contribution, the progress rate of the construction of the joint venture; the conditions and procedure for assignment of capital;
4. The list of main equipment and materials needed to establish the joint venture; products and their outlets; the ratio of foreign currency and Vietnamese currency to be collected. In case of the production of import substitution goods, the mode of payments must be expressly stated;
5. The duration of the joint venture, termination and dissolution of the joint venture;
6. The procedure for settlement of disputes between the joint venture partners, arbitration body and applicable law in cases of disputes;
7. Responsibilities of the partners in the execution of the joint venture contract;
8. The validity of the joint venture contract.

Article 22

The charter of the joint venture shall contain the following main items:

1. Nationalities, addresses and authorized representatives of the joint venture partners;

2. Name, address and business activities of the joint venture;
3. The investment capital, the legal capital; ratio of contribution to the legal capital and the progress rate of contribution to the legal capital;
4. The number, composition, responsibilities, rights, and the office term of the Board of Management, General Director and Deputy General Directors of the joint venture;
5. The representative of the joint venture before the law—courts, arbitration bodies and state authorities of Vietnam;
6. The principles governing financial matters, accounting and statistical systems; insurance of assets of the joint venture.
7. The rate of profit and loss sharing between the joint venture partners;
8. Duration of the joint venture, termination and dissolution of the joint venture;
9. Labor relations in the joint venture.
10. Training plan in regard to managerial officials, technical and business personnel and workers;
11. Procedure for amendments to the charter of the joint venture.

Article 23

1. Within three months upon receipt of the application for an investment license, the State Committee for Cooperation and Investment shall notify the joint venture partners of its decision;
2. In case the State Committee for Cooperation and Investment requires the joint venture partners to provide additional documents or to amend certain clauses of the contract and/or the charter, and the feasibility study, it shall send a written request to this effect to the partners within one month from the date of receipt of the application....

Article 24

The joint venture contract shall become effective and the joint venture shall have the status of a juridical person from the date of issuance of the investment license and certificate of registration of the charter of the joint venture....

Article 25

Any amendments to the joint venture contract as may be agreed upon by the joint venture partners shall not become valid until it is approved by the State Committee for Cooperation and Investment....

Article 27

The legal capital must be at least equivalent to thirty percent of the investment capital of the joint venture. In special cases, the proportion of legal capital over the investment capital may be lower than thirty percent but it must be approved by the State Committee for Cooperation and Investment.

The capital contribution of one or more foreign partners shall be agreed upon by the joint venture partners, but it shall not be lower than thirty percent of the legal capital of the joint venture....

Article 28

The legal capital may be contributed once in full by the joint venture partners at the time of establishment of the joint venture or by installments over a reasonable period agreed upon between the partners.

The mode for capital contribution and progress rate of capital contribution shall have to be prescribed in the joint venture contract in accordance with the feasibility study;

The State Committee for Cooperation and Investment shall have the authority to withdraw the investment license in case the joint venture partners fail to keep the progress rate of capital contribution as committed themselves without legitimate reasons.

Article 29

In the course of operations, the joint venture is not allowed to decrease its legal capital. Any increase of the investment capital and/or the legal capital or a change of the ratio of capital contribution shall be subject to the decision of the Board of Management of the joint venture and must be approved by the State Committee for Cooperation and Investment....

Article 31

1. The highest management body of the joint venture is its Board of Management;
2. The number of members of the Board of Management, the distribution of the Board membership to each partner, the nomination of the members of the Board of Management, the Director General and Deputy Directors General shall be determined in accordance with Article 12 of the Foreign Investment Law....

Article 32

1. The Board of Management shall convene at least one meeting per annum....
2. Any meeting of the Board of Management shall require the attendance of at least two-thirds of the members....

Article 33

1. The Board of Management shall have the authority to make decisions on matters of the joint venture. A decision on any matters set out below shall be made by the members of the Board of Management on the principle of unanimity:
   - Production and business plan of the joint venture in each year and in the long term, its budgets and borrowings;
   - Amendments and supplements to the charter of the joint venture;

Appendix A

- Nomination and dismissal of the Chairman of the Board of Management, the Director General, the First Deputy Director General and the chief accountant;

2. Other decisions made by the Board of Management shall be valid only if they are approved by two-thirds of the Board members present:

3. If matters stated in clause 1 of this article are not agreed upon by the members of the Board of Management on the principle of unanimity and may cause damage to the operations of the joint venture, the Board of Management may choose one of the following options:

- Settling the matter at a dispute settlement council. The dispute settlement council shall be established in agreement between joint venture partners....
- Asking the State Committee for Cooperation and Investment to act as the arbitration body to settle the dispute....
- Dissolving the joint venture....

Article 35

1. The duration of a joint venture shall be agreed upon between joint venture partners in the joint venture contract and shall be in accordance with provisions of Article 15 of the Foreign Investment Law, and must be approved by the State Committee for Cooperation and Investment....

Article 36

In case the joint venture partners agree to extend the duration of a joint venture as stated in the investment license, they shall file an application to this effect with the State Committee for Cooperation and Investment for consideration and approval at least six months prior to the expiry of the duration of the joint venture.

Within 30 days upon receipt of the application, the State

Committee for Cooperation and Investment shall notify the joint venture partners of its decision. If the application is approved, the joint venture partners may continue their operations without having to renew their registration.

Article 37

A joint venture may terminate its operations and be dissolved prior to its expiry date stated in the investment license in the following cases:

1. The joint venture partners fail to execute the contract due to certain reasons;
2. Failure by one or both partners to discharge his or her obligations stated in the contract....
3. The losses of the joint venture are such that it is no longer in a position to pursue its operations.
4. Other cases for dissolution provided for in the joint venture contract....

CHAPTER IV

Enterprises with 100% Foreign Capital

Article 43

An enterprise with 100 percent foreign capital is the one being wholly owned by a foreign organization or an individual, established in Vietnam and fully managed by that organization or individual and bears full responsibility of its business results.

Article 44

An enterprise with 100 percent foreign capital shall be established as a limited liability company and is a Vietnamese juridical person;

An enterprise with 100 percent foreign capital shall not be established until an investment license and a certificate of registration of its charter is granted to it by the State Committee for Cooperation and Investment....

Appendix A

Article 45

The duration of an enterprise with 100 percent foreign capital shall be the same as provided for the joint venture in Article 35 of this decree.

Article 46

An application submitted to the State Committee for Cooperation and Investment for issuance of an investment license...shall be accompanied by the following documents:

1. Charter of the enterprise;
2. Necessary information relating to the legal status and financial capacity of the foreign investor;
3. A feasibility study....

Article 47

The legal capital shall be at least 30 percent of the invested capital of the enterprise....

In its process of operations, an enterprise with 100 percent foreign capital shall not decrease its legal capital. An increase of such capital shall be decided by the enterprise itself but it must be approved by the State Committee for Cooperation and Investment....

Article 48

The issuance of investment license to an enterprise with 100 percent foreign capital shall proceed with the same order and procedure as for a joint venture enterprise....

Article 51

The nonresident owner of the enterprise shall appoint a duly authorized representative residing in Vietnam. The latter shall have to register with the State Committee for Cooperation and Investment....

Chapter V

Export Processing Zones, Export Processing Enterprises, Building-Operating-Transferring Contracts

Article 54

The Government of Vietnam encourages the establishment of joint venture companies between Vietnamese partner/partners and foreign investor/investors to build and operate infrastructural works in the Export Processing Zones.

Article 55

The building-operating-transferring (BOT) contracts are agreements between the investor/investors and the authorized Government agency/agencies to build infrastructures such as bridges, roads, ports, power plants, etc. in Vietnam.

BOT contracts may be carried out with 100 percent foreign capital or in combination with the capital contributed by the Government of Vietnam and/or of Vietnamese organizations or individuals. The investors shall be responsible for building and operating the infrastructures within a given period of time to recover their invested capital and make reasonable profits and transfer them thereafter without any compensation to the Government of Vietnam....

Chapter IX

Financial Matters

Article 66

Enterprises with foreign invested capital and business cooperation foreign partners shall have to pay corporate income tax at 25 percent of the profit made except the privileged cases of investment incentives stated in Article 67 of this Decree.

Appendix A

In respect of projects for exploitation of oil and gas and some rare and precious natural resources, the corporate income tax rate may be higher than 25 percent of the profit made depending on the nature and characteristics of each project.

Article 67

The rates of corporate income tax in privileged cases for investment incentives are as follows:

1. 20 percent for projects having two of the following requirements:
   - Employing 500 or more workers;
   - Using advanced technology;
   - Exporting at least 80 percent of the products;
   - Having legal capital or contributed capital in business cooperation amounting to USD $10 million or more;
2. 15 percent for projects of:
   - Infrastructural construction;
   - Exploitation of natural resources (except oil and gas and rare, precious resources);
   - Heavy industry;
   - Growing perennial industrial plants;
   - Investment in the mountains and regions of harsh natural and socio-economic conditions;
   - No-compensation transfer of projects (including hotels) to Vietnam when the project terminates.
3. 10 percent for enterprises with foreign invested capital carrying out projects of:
   - Building infrastructures in the mountains and regions of harsh natural and socio-economic conditions;
   - Afforestation;
   - Special importance.

Article 68

The tax rates stated in Article 67 shall not apply with hotel projects (except investments in the mountains and regions of harsh natural and socio-economic conditions, or no-compensation transfer of properties to Vietnam upon termination), and projects in banking, finance, insurance, accounting service, auditing service, and trading.

Article 69

The reduction or exemption of corporate income tax for enterprises with foreign invested capital shall be as follows:

1. The projects referred to in Article 66 of this Decree may be examined for income tax exemption in one year since profits are made and reduction by 50 percent in two subsequent years at most;
2. The projects referred to in paragraph 1 of Article 67 may be examined for income tax exemption in two years since profits are made and reduction by 50 percent in three subsequent years at most;
3. The projects referred to in paragraph 2 of Article 67 may be examined for income tax exemption in two years since profits are made and reduction by 50 percent in four subsequent years;
4. The projects referred to in paragraph 3 of Article 67 may be exempted from income tax in four years since profits are made and enjoy a reduction of 50 percent in four subsequent years....

Article 70

The foreign organizations and individuals shall pay a tax on overseas remittance of profits at the following rates:

1. Five percent of the overseas remitted profits for the foreign organizations and individuals having contributed legal capital or business cooperation capital of USD $10 million and over;
2. Seven percent of the overseas remitted profits for the foreign organizations and individuals having

contributed legal capital and business cooperation capital of USD $5 million and over;
3. 10 percent of the overseas remitted profits for the cases apart from those stated in paragraphs 1 and 2 of this Article.

Article 71

The State Committee for Cooperation and Investment shall made decisions on specific tax rates and time of their levy and the cases of corporate income tax exemption or reduction prescribed....

Article 72

Any foreign organization or individual that re-invests their share of profits for a period of three years or more shall be entitled to a refund of the tax paid for the profits being re-invested....

Article 75

For business cooperation contracts, the method of assessing business results shall be determined by the State Committee for Cooperation and Investment to be suitable to the type of cooperation and as proposed by the partners concerned....

Article 76

A foreign-invested enterprise and the business cooperation partners may be entitled to import tax exemption in the following cases:
1. The imported machinery, equipment, spare parts and production business facilities (including transport means) and other materials to invest in the capital construction of the enterprise or to be used as fixed assets of the contractual business cooperation;
2. Raw materials, spare parts, accessories and other materials imported for the production of goods. These imported articles shall be subject to a tempo-

rary import duty payments but a tax refund respective to the exported goods shall be made;

3. Invention patents, technical know-how, industrial processes, technical services, etc. contributed by the foreign partners as part of the legal capital of the foreign-invested enterprise or the initial capital of the business cooperation shall be exempted from all taxes related to the technology transfer....

Chapter X

Foreign Exchange Control

Article 80

All capital funds and revenues of an enterprise with foreign invested capital in foreign and Vietnamese currencies must be deposited in accounts opened at Vietnam Bank or at a joint Vietnamese-foreign bank or at the branch of a foreign bank in Vietnam.

All revenues and expenditures of the enterprise shall be transacted through these accounts. The foreign partners in a contractual business cooperation may open similar accounts as stipulated above. In special cases, if the creditor expects the debtor to open accounts for loans at banks in a foreign country, the enterprise is entitled to do so with the approval from the State Bank of Vietnam....

Article 83

1. Foreign economic organizations and individuals investing in Vietnam have the right to remit abroad:
    - The profits accrued from business operations;
    - Revenues from services and technology transferred;
    - The principal and interests of foreign loans made in the course of operations;
    - The invested capital;
    - All other sums of money and assets in their legal ownership....

Article 84

The foreigners working for a foreign-invested enterprise or contractual business cooperation shall have the right to remit abroad in foreign currencies their salaries and wages and other legal incomes after deduction of their due income tax and other expenses....

CHAPTER XII

Customs, Immigration, Residence, and Communications

Article 91

Personal effects of the foreign partner of a foreign-invested enterprise or contractual business cooperation and the foreigner working for an investment project shall be given preferential treatment on importation in accordance to the current regulations.

Article 92

The General Department of Customs shall grant import-export licenses to the personal effects of foreigners as indicated in Article 91 of this Decree.

Article 93

The foreigner entering Vietnam to investigate and prepare an investment shall be granted a multiple-entry visa valid for three months and extendible very three months.

Article 94

The foreigner participating in an investment project (including his/her personal help) shall be granted a multiple-entry visa valid for one year and extendible every year corresponding to the terms of the contract, with due consideration of the time required for the dissolution of the enterprise or termination of the contract....

B

SAMPLE APPLICATION FORMS FOR DOING BUSINESS IN VIETNAM

Regardless of the form your business activity in Vietnam takes, you will be required to apply to the Vietnamese government. Applications for the establishment of representative offices in Vietnam must be submitted to the Ministry of Trade and Tourism. Applications for business cooperation, joint venture, and 100% foreign-ownership projects are submitted to the State Committee for Cooperation and Investment (SCCI).

In addition, the feasibility study figures heavily in the approval process for the SCCI-related investments. The government has issued specific guidelines for the preparation of the feasibility study.

The following are sample application forms as well as government specifications for the feasibility study. Other sources include SCCI publications: "Guidance on Preparation of Documents for Foreign Direct Investment Projects in Vietnam" (Statistical Publishing House, Hanoi, 1994) and "Content of the Feasibility Study." Both are available for purchase from the SCCI's Hanoi or Ho Chi Minh City offices.

Also, Deloitte Touche Tohmatsu's pamphlet "Vietnam Business Profile" is available for purchase through the firm's Hong Kong office (tel: 852-545-5811; fax: 852-854-0076).

REPRESENTATIVE OFFICE

[Letterhead of your company]

To His Excellency the Minister of Trade and Tourism
Socialist Republic of Vietnam, Hanoi

Application for Setting Up of Resident Representative Office in the Socialist Republic of Vietnam

Excellency,

_____[company name]_____ presents its compliments to His Excellency the Minister and has the honor to apply for His Excellency to set up its Resident Representative office in [city] under the following description:

1. Full designation of the office:
2. Number of staff: ____ members, including:
   Staff members from foreign countries:
   To assume the following assignments:

   Staff members recruited in Vietnam:
   To assume the following assignments:
3. Areas of activities:
4. Duration of the office:

We undertake that in the course of its activities in Vietnam, the Resident Representative Office and its staff members shall strictly abide by the laws in force in the Socialist Republic of Vietnam and shall run its activities as permitted by the Ministry.

Yours Respectfully,

President

Enclosures:

- Register book or certificate of incorporation together with its charter (photocopied; translated into English, French, or Russian; and certified by a notary public).
- Profile of the company in Vietnamese and translated into English, French, or Russian. (Profile must include name, nationality, address, years of establishment, number of employees, authorized capital, main shareholders, registered business activities, annual turnover for last three years, related bankers, and detailed relations and activities with Vietnamese partners.)

Additional enclosures may be required by the Ministry of Trade and Tourism:

- Banker's certification of company's financial status.
- Copies of contracts and agreements concluded with the projects envisaged for development with Vietnamese partners.

BUSINESS COOPERATION LICENSE

Investment Application for Licensing a Business Cooperation Contract

Date: _____

TO: The State Committee for Cooperation and Investment

An investment application under the Foreign Investment Law of Vietnam is herewith being submitted by the undersigned to the Socialist Republic of Vietnam through the State Committee for Cooperation and Investment.

Particulars regarding the proposed Business Cooperation as well as the requested investment incentives and related data/documentation are described herein and submitted:

I. Vietnamese party or parties:

Name of company and ministerial relationship:

Head office address and phone/fax:

Main business activities:
Permit number:
Issued by:
Authorized representative:

II. Foreign party or parties:
Name, address, and phone/fax:
Main activities of business:
Business permit:
Financial status:
Bank and account number:
Authorized representative:
Position, nationality, and permanent address:

III. We wish to apply for a business license in order to implement the Business Cooperation Contract signed on _____. (Contract is enclosed and includes type of business activity, duration, scope of cooperation as indicated by anticipated annual output and/or turnover, description of transferred technology, environmental protection measures, market for products, ratio of business-gain sharing of the parties, and responsibilities of the respective parties.)

IV. We wish to apply for the following Investment Incentives:

V. The documents enclosed with this application comprise: Certification concerning judicial person status as well as company's certified annual report and/or banker's reference from an internationally acceptable financial institution;

Legalized power of attorney for signing this application and the business cooperation contract;

The economic and technical feasibility studies;

The surveyor's inspection report regarding used or secondhand equipment.

Vietnamese Party	Foreign Party
[Signature, seal]	[signature, seal]

Appendix B

JOINT VENTURE LICENSE
Investment Application for Licensing a Joint Venture

Date: _____

TO: The State Committee for Cooperation and Investment

An investment application under the Foreign Investment Law of Vietnam is herewith being submitted by the undersigned to the Socialist Republic of Vietnam through the State Committee for Cooperation and Investment.

Particulars regarding the proposed Joint Venture as well as the requested investment incentives and related data/documentation are described herein and submitted:

I. Vietnamese party or parties:
  Name of company and ministerial relationship:
  Head office address and phone/fax:
  Main business activities:
  Permit number:
  Issued by:
  Authorized representative:

II. Foreign party or parties:
  Name, address, and phone/fax:
  Main activities of business:
  Business permit:
  Financial status:
  Bank and account number:
  Authorized representative:
  Position, nationality and permanent address:

III. We wish to apply for an investment license in order to implement the Joint Venture Contract signed on _____.

IV. We wish to apply for the following Investment Incentives:

V. The documents enclosed with this application comprise:

The joint venture contract;

The joint venture charter/articles of association;

Certification concerning juridical person status as well as the company's certified annual report and/or banker's reference from an international accepted financial institution;

Legalized power of attorney for signing this application and the joint venture contract;

The economic and technical feasibility studies;

The surveyor's inspection report regarding used or secondhand equipment.

Vietnamese Party   Foreign Party
[signature, seal]   [Signature, seal]

Guidance for a Joint Venture Contract and Charter as Issued by the State Committee for Cooperation and Investment

Contract

Article 1:
1. Objectives of the joint venture company
2. Name of company and transaction name if different

Article 2:
1. Address of head office, production factory, branches, and representative offices
2. Production capabilities of facilities
3. Extent of marketing and expected sales both foreign and domestic

Article 3:
1. Total invested capital of joint venture
2. Total legal capital, percent, and type contributed by each party

Appendix B

3. Loans and credit anticipated

Article 4:

1. Schedule of contribution of capital by each party

Article 5:

1. Rules for informing parties if capital contribution is delayed

Article 6:

1. Program for increasing capital contribution of Vietnamese party

Article 7:

1. Term of duration of joint venture contract

Article 8:

1. Schedule for importation of building materials and construction

2. Schedule for importation of equipment and machinery

3. Schedule for trial production

4. Schedule for official production

Article 9:

1. Detail of other responsibilities of each partner

Article 10:

1. Formula for sharing the net profits

Article 11:

1. Specific method chosen for resolving partner disputes

Article 12:

1. Provision for dissolution ahead of schedule

Charter

In addition to information contained in the joint venture contract, the joint venture charter must contain the following: members of the Board of Management, the board's officers, and their respective appointing powers; specific currency to be used; name of bank to be used; accounting system agreed upon; depreciation rate of fixed assets; and name and address of insurance organization protecting the assets.

100% FOREIGN-OWNED ENTERPRISE LICENSE

Investment Application for Licensing an Enterprise with 100% Foreign-Owned Capital

Date: _____

TO: State Committee for Cooperation and Investment

An investment application under the Foreign Investment Law of Vietnam herewith is being submitted by the undersigned to the Socialist Republic of Vietnam through the State Committee for Cooperation and Investment.

Particulars regarding the proposed business cooperation as well as the requested investment incentives and related data/documentation are described herein and submitted:

I. Name of company wishes to be issued an investment license in order to establish in Vietnam an enterprise with 100% foreign-owned capital in accordance with the charter attached herewith.

II. We wish to apply for the following investment incentives:

III. The documents enclosed with this application comprise:

The charter of the enterprise with 100% foreign-owned capital. (Charter must include the following: major business-production objectives; total capital, fixed, working, and legal; loans; quantity and source of supply of main materials; anticipated production market; duration of operation; insurance of assets; Vietnamese and expatriate labor force; manage-

Appendix B

ment structure; schedule of implementation; and environmental protection measures.)

Certification concerning juridical person status, as well as the company's certified annual report and/or banker's reference from an internationally acceptable financial institution

Legalized power of attorney for signing this application and the charter of the proposed enterprise

The economic and technical feasibility studies

The appointed survey's inspection report concerning used or secondhand equipment

The Investor
[signature and seal]

CONTENTS OF THE FEASIBILITY STUDY
(In accordance with the Joint Circular Dated November 9, 1991, of the State Planning Commission and the Ministry of Building)

The content of the feasibility study shall include:

1. Justification for the investment project, including background and analysis based on investigation of market, investment targets, market analysis, and the selected products or groups of products.
2. Forms of investment and production capacity, including why the form of investment was chosen and whether new facilities for production will be built or existing facilities refurbished.
3. Production program and supplying demand, including production capacity and schedule; requirements for raw materials and how they will be sources; need for electricity, water supply, and communications; and a marketing program.
4. Variants on locations and sites, including analysis of site needs and characteristics of possible sites and

economic and social impacts and benefits of potential sites.

5. Technology and technological processes, including analysis of production process from standpoint of technological sophistication, content of, and technology transfer, ecological problems and their resolution, and list of specific equipment to be used and total cost.

6. Construction and installation, including construction standards, method, schedule, and architectural design; materials and machinery needed.

7. Production management and manpower planning, including organization plan for management; workforce requirements and expenses; and expenses for overhead, administration, management, and plant operation.

8. Economic and financial analysis, including amount, source, and distribution plan of capital and estimate of timetable for capital recovery and breakeven point.

9. Organization of implementation, including concluding statements and proposals and justifications for preferential treatment.

SOURCES

BOOKS, STUDIES, AND OFFICIAL PUBLICATIONS

Burke, Frederick R., and David Howell. *Vietnam: A Legal Brief.* Hanoi: The State Political Publishing House, 1993. (bilingual publication)
Cummings, Joe, and Daniel Robinson. *Vietnam, Laos & Cambodia: A Travel Survival Kit.* Hawthorn, Australia: Lonely Planet Publications, 1991.
Deloitte Touche Tohmatsu International. *Vietnam Business Profile.* Hong Kong: Deloitte Touche Tohmatsu, 1993.
Englemann, Larry. *Tears Before the Rain: An Oral History of the Fall of South Vietnam.* New York: Oxford University Press, 1990.
Grub, Phillip Donald, and Nguyen Xuan Oanh. *Vietnam: The New Investment Frontier in Southeast Asia.* Singapore: Times Academic Press, 1992.
Hanoi Post and Telecommunications and Worldcorp Holdings Ltd. *Hanoi Telephone Directory and Yellow Pages.* Singapore: Worldcorp, 1993. (bilingual publication)
Hiebert, Murray. *Vietnam Notebook.* Hong Kong: Review Publishing Company, Ltd., 1993.

Ho Chi Minh City Post and Telecommunications and Worldcorp Holdings Ltd. *Ho Chi Minh City Telephone Directory and Yellow Pages.* Singapore: Worldcorp, 1993. (bilingual publication)

Hong Kong Trade Development Council. *Vietnam: Market Prospects and Investment Environment.* Hong Kong: Hong Kong Trade Development Council, 1992.

Infocus Ltd. *Managing Doi Moi: A Dialogue between Vietnam's Government and Foreign Investors.* Hong Kong: Infocus Ltd., June 1993. (conference papers)

Jones, John R. *Guide to Vietnam.* Edison, N.J.: Hunter Publishing, 1989.

Michener, James A. *The Voice of Asia.* New York: Random House, 1951.

Ministry of Finance. *Regulations on the Depreciation of Fixed Assets Applied for Foreign Invested Enterprises and Sales Fees.* Hanoi: Government publication, 1992. (bilingual publication)

———. *Regulations on the Lease of Land, Water and Sea Surfaces for Foreign Investment in Vietnam.* Hanoi: Government publication, 1990. (bilingual publication)

National Assembly. *Law on Amendment of and Addition to a Number of Articles of the Law on Foreign Investment in Vietnam.* Hanoi: Government publication, 1993. (bilingual publication)

Nixon, Richard. *No More Vietnams.* New York: Arbor House, 1985.

Pacific Basin Research Institute. *Toward a Market Economy in Vietnam: Economic Reforms and Development Strategies for the 21st Century.* Rockville, Md.: Pacific Basin Research Institute, 1993.

Price Waterhouse. *Vietnam: A Guide for the Investor.* Hong Kong: Price Waterhouse, 1993.

Prime Minister's Office. *Decision of the Prime Minister on the Amendment of an Addition to the Import and Export Tariffs.* Hanoi: Government publication, 1994. (bilingual publication)

SGV Group and the Foreign Investment Service Company. *Doing Business in Vietnam.* Manila: SGV and Co., 1993.

Shoesmith, Thomas M. *Vietnam: The New Frontier.* San Diego: Baker and McKenzie, 1993.

State Committee for Cooperation and Investment. *Foreign Direct Investment in Vietnam.* Hanoi: Government publication, 1993.

———. *Guidance on Preparation of Documents for Foreign Direct Investment Projects in Vietnam.* Hanoi: Statistical Publishing House, 1994. (bilingual publication)

———. *Legal Writings on Foreign Investment in Vietnam.* Hanoi: Government publication, 1992. (bilingual publication)

———. *List of Licensed Projects from 1988 to 1992.* Ho Chi Minh City: Government publication, 1993. (bilingual publication)

———. *List of Licensed Projects in 1993.* Ho Chi Minh City: Government publication, 1994. (bilingual publication)

---. *List of Projects.* Hanoi: Government Publication, 1992. (bilingual publication)

State Planning Commission and Ministry of Building. *Content of the Feasibility Study.* Hanoi: Government publication, 1991. (bilingual publication)

Timberman, Thomas M.F. *Vietnam: The No BS Business Guide.* Washington, D.C.: LOI, 1994.

United Nations Development Programme. *Briefing Note: Socialist Republic of Vietnam.* Hanoi: United Nations Development Program, 1993.

---. *Directory of Institutions and Government Officials of the Socialist Republic of Vietnam.* Hanoi: United Nations Development Programme, 1994.

Youth Advertising House and Annboli Co., Ltd. *Vietnam Opportunities.* Hong Kong: Longman Group, 1992.

ARTICLES AND PERIODICALS

Author's Note: As discussed in chapter 14, the most comprehensive and timely information resource on business developments in Vietnam is the *Vietnam Investment Review,* a weekly English-language business newspaper published in Hanoi by the government's State Committee for Cooperation and Investment and its foreign partner, Vietnam Investment Review Ltd. The more than 150 issues published to date chronicle the opening of the Vietnamese economy to the outside world in rich detail. In preparing this book, I have relied heavily on the newspaper's reporting. Issues of particular importance follow.

Vietnam Investment Review: Vol. 3, No. 103 (Oct. 4–10, 1993); No. 104 (Oct. 11–17, 1993); No. 109 (Nov. 15–21, 1993); No. 110 (Nov. 22–28, 1993); No. 111 (Nov. 23–Dec. 5, 1993); No. 113 (Dec. 13–19, 1993); No. 114 (Dec. 20–26, 1993); No. 115 (Dec. 27–Jan. 2, 1994).

Vietnam Investment Review: Vol. 4, No. 116 (Jan. 3–9, 1994); No. 117, (Jan. 10–16, 1994); No. 118 (Jan. 17–23, 1994); No. 119 (Jan. 24–30, 1994); No. 120 (Jan. 31–Feb. 6, 1994); No. 123 (Feb. 21–27, 1994); No. 124 (Feb. 28–Mar. 6, 1994); No. 125 (Mar. 7–13, 1994); No. 126 (Mar. 14–20, 1994); No. 127 (Mar. 21–27, 1994); No. 128 (Mar. 28–Apr. 3, 1994); No. 132 (Apr. 21–May 1, 1994).

Other Articles and Periodicals

Associated Press. "Airlines Undeterred by Vietnam Political Snags." *Los Angeles Times,* 25 April 1994, D3.

———. "US Hailed for Ending Vietnam Ban." *The (Bangkok) Nation,* 5 February 1994, 1, 3.

———. "Vietnam Refugee Finds New Future in Homeland." *Los Angeles Times,* 14 March 1994, D3.

Bangkok Post. "Asians Expect More Competition." *Bangkok Post,* 6 February 1994, 17.

Beck, Simon, and Mark Evans. "HK Faces Vietnam Challenge from US." *South China Morning Post,* 3 February 1994, 1, 5, 14, 15.

Brownmiller, Susan. "Saigon Days, Hanoi Nights." *Los Angeles Times Magazine,* 6 February 1994, 10–14, 38–40.

Business News Indochina, April 1994.

Cathay Pacific. "Good Morning, Vietnam." *Discovery,* November 1991, 38–162.

Chamber of Commerce and Industry in Vietnam. *Vietnam Foreign Trade,* Vol. 35, No. 4 (1993); Vol. 36, No. 1 (1994).

Chanda, Nayan. "Money Pit: Hanoi Ponders Another Currency Devaluation." *Far Eastern Economic Review,* 14 April 1994, 64.
Chau, Le Van. "Prospects for Vietnam's Economic Development." *Vietnam Banking Review,* March 1994, 1–2.
Cuc, Nguyen Xuan. "Foreign Investment Panorama in Six Years." *Business Vietnam,* 31 March–30 April 1994.
Fallows, James. "Shut Out." *TAB: The Journal of the American Chamber of Commerce in Thailand,* March–April 1991, 32–36.
Far Eastern Economic Review. "Editorial: Ending America's Vietnam Syndrome." *Far Eastern Economic Review,* 7 January 1993, 5.
Gaines, James R. "Back onto the World Stage." *Time,* 11 April 1994, 28.
Gardner, Janet. "Green versus Greenbacks." *Choices,* Vol. 2, No. 2, 8–9.
Genovese, Mathilde L. "Navigating through Vietnam's Foreign Investment Process." *Foreign Trade Association of Southern California,* 17 March 1994.
Handley, Paul. "River of Promise." *Far Eastern Economic Review,* 16 September 1993, 68–70.
Harvey, John M. "Indochina Update." *Ernst & Young,* December 1993.
Hiebert, Murray. "Against the Grain: Inefficiencies Hobble Vietnam's Rice Exports." *Far Eastern Economic Review,* 14 April 1994, 66.
———. "Drinks All Round: The Battle Is on for Vietnam's Beer Market." *Far Eastern Economic Review,* 17 March 1994, 55.
———. "Food or Forests?" *Far Eastern Economic Review,* 7 April 1994, 64.
———. "Good Morning Vietnam: US Declares Peace through Trade." *Far Eastern Economic Review,* 17 February 1994, 14–17.
———. "He Hit the Ground Cycling." *Far Eastern Economic Review,* 7 January 1993, 50.
———. "Industrial Disease: Strikes on the Rise at Foreign-Owned Factories." *Far Eastern Economic Review,* 2 September 1993, 16–17.
———. "Late into the Fray." *Far Eastern Economic Review,* 7 January 1993, 48–49.
———. "Obstacle Course." *Far Eastern Economic Review,* 5 September 1991, 64–65.
———. "The Rise of Saigon." *Far Eastern Economic Review,* 5 September 1991, 62–64.
———. "Vietnam's New Entrepreneurs." *Far Eastern Economic Review,* 31 March 1994, 62–64.
Ho, Luu Bich. "Vietnam's Economy up to the Year 2000." *Vietnam Commentary,* May–June, 6–8.
Hoan, Le Ngoc. "Transport and Communication." *Vietnam Commentary,* July–August 1992, 2–8.
Hong Kong Trade Development Council. "Post-Embargo Vietnam: Opportunities and Challenges." *New Market Search,* April 1994, 1–6.

Janssen, Peter. "The Best Is Yet to Come." *Asian Business,* July 1993, 28-32.

———. "Divided by Development." *Asian Business,* July 1993, 33-36.

Jehl, Douglas. "Clinton Drops 19-Year Ban on U.S. Trade with Vietnam." *New York Times,* 4 February 1994, 1, 6.

Johnson, Tim. "Vietnamese Coffee Needs Designer Image for Japan." *Mainichi Daily News,* 30 January 1994, 5.

Kanwerayotin, Supapohn. "Investors Urge Search for VN Business Synergies." *Bangkok Post,* 5 February 1994, 1.

———. "VN Businessmen Cautiously Welcome End to Embargo." *Bangkok Post,* 5 February 1994, 17.

Keatley, Robert. "Two Firms Hope for Success in Vietnam by Dispensing Advice to U.S. Investors." *Wall Street Journal,* 29 April 1994, B6.

Kotkin, Joel. "An Emerging Asian Tiger: The Vietnamese Connection." *Los Angeles Times,* 24 April 1994, M1, 6.

Lam, Andrew. "Dragon in a Basket." *Choices,* Vol. 2, No. 2, 4-8.

———. "Love, Money, Prison, Sin, Revenge." *Los Angeles Times Magazine,* 13 March 1994, 24-26, 28, 30, 56-58.

Lyons, Don. "Topping Off for $23m Complex." *South China Morning Post,* 13 April 1994, P2.

Malhotra, Angelina. "Death of a Port." *Asia, Inc.,* April 1994, 14-17.

Mathewson, Ruth. "Hai Phong Lures HK Industries." *South China Morning Post,* 10 April 1994, 3.

———. "Raising Vietnam." *South China Morning Post,* 10 April 1994, 12.

Murray, Marjorie. "Vietnam on the Block." *California Lawyer,* January 1994, 20-22.

Ngo, Nguyen Truong. "The Renovation of the Banking System." *Vietnam Commentary,* May-June 1992, 9-11.

Nguyen, Hoang. "The State-Owned Enterprises." *Vietnam Commentary,* March-April 1992, 13-15.

Phuoc, Nguyen Van. "Agriculture and Food Industry." *Vietnam Commentary* July-August 1922, 9-11.

Rajaretnam, M. "Doing Business in Vietnam: A New Role for Singapore." *Vietnam Commentary,* March-April 1992, 2-8.

Reuters. "Pepsi Fires First Shot in Cola War." *Bangkok Post,* 6 February 1994, 17.

———. "Thailand Hails End of Embargo." *Bangkok Post,* 5 February 1994, 1, 3, 4, 6, 15, 17, 22.

Richter, Paul and Michael Ross. "Clinton Lifts Vietnam Embargo to Resolve the Fate of MIAs." *Los Angeles Times,* 4 February 1994, 1, 6.

Robinson, James W. "Vietnam a Market of Great Potential for US Businesses." *Orange County Register,* 2 December 1990, C1.

Rogers, David. "Bouncing Back: Brick Houses and Soda on Ice Bear Witness to Vietnam's Revival." *Wall Street Journal,* 3 January 1994, 1, 4.

Sources

Saigon Times, No. 133, 21–27 April 1994.
Schoenberger, Karl. "Champing at the Bit: U.S. Firms Are Eager to Get into Vietnam with Lifting of Trade Embargo." *Los Angeles Times*, 4 February 1994, D1, 12.
Seto, Benjamin. "Grape Group Testing Vietnam." *Fresno Bee*, 5 April 1994, A12.
Stanley, Bruce. "Surfing Returns to China Beach." *Japan Times*, 11 October 1993, 20.
Sutter, Robert G. "Vietnam in Transition: Implications for U.S. Policy." *Congressional Research Service Report or Congress*, 4 March 1989.
Tai, Nguyen. "Infrastructure Development: The Need in Vietnam's Cities." *Vietnam Commentary*, May–June 1992, 12–15.
Tempest, Rone. "French Launch Verbal War over Vietnam Visit." *Los Angeles Times*, 16 February 1993, H6.
Thao, Tran Dinh. "Post-Embargo Economy at a Glance." *Vietnam Courier*, 17–23 April 1994, 1, 4
U.S. Chamber of Commerce. "Statement on Prospects for Normalization of Relations with Vietnam." 25 April 1991.
Vietnam Airlines. *Heritage*, March/April 1994.
Vietnam Import Export Trade Letter, Vol. 1, No. 1 (15 April 1993).
Vietnam News. No. 972 (Apr. 17, 1994); No. 973 (Apr. 18, 1994); No. 974 (Apr. 19, 1994); No. 975 (Apr. 20, 1994); No. 976 (Apr. 21, 1994).
Wain, Barry. "Vietnam Publicity Hype over Economy Masks a Passel of Problems." *Wall Street Journal*, 20 May 1994, A5A.
Wall Street Journal. "U.S. Firms Ready for Lifting of Embargo on Vietnam, but Some Obstacles Remain." *Wall Street Journal*, 3 February 1994, A2, 8.
Wallace, Charles P. "Vietnamese Celebrate Trade Embargo's End." *Los Angeles Times*, 6 February 1994, 1, 9.
_____. "Vietnamese Officials Eager for U.S. Firms to Join Search for Oil." *Los Angeles Times*, 26 January 1994, D4.
Wei, Tan Chee. "Vietnamese Consumer Prefers Imported Branded Goods: Poll." *Singapore Straits Times*, 15 February 1993.
Worthy, Ford S. "Getting Ready to Get into Vietnam." *Fortune*, 6 April 1992, 106–109.
Xuan, Dau Ngoc. "The New Frontier for Foreign Investments." *Vietnam Commentary*, May–June 1992, 2–5.

Index

advertising industry, 51
agribusiness, 48–49
American Chamber of Commerce in Hong Kong, 177–178
auto industry, 48
aviation industry, 46–47

Bagnall, David, 54–55
Bank of America, 180
banking, 51–52, 166–117
boat people, 13
build-operate-transfer projects, 65, 258
business cooperation contract, 63, 246–250

Charlton, Kathleen, 97
Chrysler, 120
Clinton, Bill, 3
Coca-cola, 4
computer industry, 47

construction industry, 43–44
consumer products, 49, 77–79
corruption, 20, 113–115
crime, 151

Da Nang, 41–42, 163
Deukmejian, George, 11
doi moi policy, 9–11, 12, 14–15
Dunkley, Ross, 29, 54, 97–98, 101, 115
DuPont, 31

embargo, 3, 10, 12
Eng, Landy, 71–72, 89
entertainment industry, 49
entrepreneurs, opportunities for, 40
Ernst & Young, 64, 179
exploratory business missions, 57–59
export processing zones, 65–66, 258

283

Far East Economic Review, 201–202
Foreign Investment Service Company (FISC), 115–130, 182
foreign investment
  application process for, 66, 68–69, 265–274
  examples of, 205–212
  U.S. companies involved in, 214–215
  Vietnamese government priorities for, 35–36
foreign investment law, 62, 225–263

Ha, Henry, 102
Ha Long bay, 164
Hanoi, 41, 103–104, 163–164
Harvey, John, 106
Ho Chi Minh City (Saigon), 38, 40, 103–104, 161–162
Ho, Paul, 101, 115
Hong Kong Trade Development Council, 73, 178
hotel accommodations, 141–142, 145–149
hotel industry, 45–46

infrastructure projects, 40, 42–43
international lending programs, 37–38

joint ventures, 63–64, 250–256

land leases and costs, 67–68
legal services, 51
legal system, 110
Little Saigon, 121

manufacturing opportunities, 44–45
marketing, 81
Mathews, Eugene, 112, 116

Ministry of Trade and Tourism, 73–74
Mobil, 119
Most Favored Nation trade status, 87–88

names, 94–96

office space, 118
oil industry, 50
100% foreign owned companies, 256–258
overseas Vietnamese (*Viet Kieu*),
  attitudes of, 121–125
  attitude of Vietnamese government towards, 125–127
  considerations for companies in hiring, 127–130
  opportunities for, 130–134

Pepsi Cola, 3
Price Waterhouse, 110, 117

Rand, Ayn, 221
representative offices, 59–61, 213–215
restaurants, 155–157

Saigon Times, 203
Saigontourist, 141, 165, 182
service industries, 51
Skadden, Arps, Slate, Meagher & From, 176, 182–3
sightseeing options, 161–165
Singapore, 11–12
smuggling, 76
State Committee for Cooperation and Investment (SCCI), 35, 62
Stonehouse, Shawna, 100

tariffs, 74–75
taxes, 118–119, 259–262

Index

telecommunications, 47–48
tourism, 45–46
trade policies, 71–76
trading companies, 184–186
trademarks, 84–87
Tu, Tran Thien, 40

U.S. Department of Commerce, 175, 187
urban planning, 51

veterans, 119–120, 164
Vietnam
  attitudes towards Americans, 57, 76–77, 159–160
  current market conditions, 16–17
  economic conditions, 3–6, 25–26
  foreign investment in, 32–34
  foreign trade of, 71–73
  government officials and ministries of, 191–199
  government owned companies, 27
  lack of political freedom, 19–20
  methods of going business in, 61–66
  mixed economy of, 26–27
  press restriction in, 21
  private sector of, 27–28
  sexual mores in, 22
  statistical profile of, 23–24
  U.S. relations with, 10–11, 187–188
Vietnamese business practices, 93–99
  business attire, 96–97
  business costs, 117
  business problems, 109
  business partners, 34–35, 67, 91–92, 115–116
  conduct in meetings, 97–99
  face, importance of, 105–106
  gifts, 96
  names, 94–96
  organizations supporting business, 174–180
  political discussions, 103
  smoking and drinking, 99–100
  women, role of, 100
Vietnam, traveling in,
  airlines, 140
  business services and communications, 151–153
  holidays, 154
  hotels, 140–142, 145–149
  immigration and customs, 143–145
  restaurants, 155–157
  sample trip and costs, 168–171
  taxis and hire cars, 145, 149–150
  time zone of Vietnam, 153
  visas, 138–139
  water, 154–155
Vietnam Business Association of Hong Kong, 178
Vietnam Chamber of Commerce and Industry, 115, 139, 180–181
Vietnam Investment Information and Consulting, 176
Vietnam Investment Review, 53–55, 202
Vietnamerica Expo '94, 9, 215–220
Vung Tau, 113

Worldcorp Holdings of Singapore, 203

ABOUT THE AUTHOR

From 1987–1993, James W. Robinson served as governor's trade representative for California Governor George Deukmejian and later as a California world trade commissioner. His accomplishments included overseeing the establishment of the state's five foreign trade and investment offices, including its Asian offices located in Tokyo and Hong Kong.

Mr. Robinson has traveled extensively throughout Vietnam and Asia, writing and speaking frequently on business opportunities in the region. He has previously served as director of executive communications for the U.S. Chamber of Commerce in Washington, D.C., and as executive assistant to U.S. Congressman Gerald Solomon of New York. As an executive with the Hannaford Company public affairs firm, he has handled assignments for clients such as Ronald Reagan, the Hong Kong Economic and Trade Office, and the Government Information

Office of Taiwan. Mr. Robinson is currently the director of communications for the California attorney general.

The author holds degrees from Middlebury College in Vermont and the University of Maryland. Previous books, all published by Prima, include *Winning Them Over* (1987), *Better Speeches in Ten Steps* (1988), and *Ross Perot Speaks Out* (1992). Mr. Robinson lives in Los Angeles and Sacramento, California.